ALL WHO
COME
ARE WELCOME

HE RECEIVES, RESTORES, REVEALS, AND REWARDS

BY
SYAVIHA MULENGYA

This book is a gift

From:_____

To:_____

On:_____

Personal Comments

_____

_____

_____

_____

_____

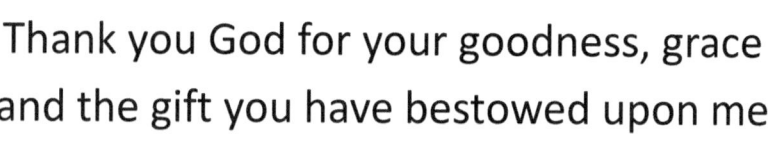

Thank you God for your goodness, grace
and the gift you have bestowed upon me

DEDICATION

- To my late parents, Samuel Mahamba and Elizabeth Vahingania, thank you for loving, listening and leading me in the ways of God.

- My brothers and sisters, Moise, Samson, Schandrack, Semu, Seriba, Yerusi, Desize, Kahambu and Katungu Mulengya, thank you for teaching me the values of hope, humility and hard work.

- To my mentors, Janine and Sid Phillips, thank you for your inspiration, instruction and information. You always encourage and believe in my vision.

- To Devin and Christine Walker, you have motivated me to serve, seek and stay close to God. Thank you for your wisdom and the great work you are doing.

- To my queen Rafiki Kavuya Syaviha, thank you for standing, supporting and serving with me in hard and good times. You are my miracle.

- To my lovely daughters, Blessed and Best and Brilliance, you always encourage, excite and enjoy my work. You are my greatest inspiration.

- To my friends and fans, you always advise, appreciate and assist me in this noble work. Thank you for the financial support.

Table of Content

INTRODUCTION

1. Calling

God's love is wide, deep, and welcoming. He doesn't wait for people to be perfect before He calls them. Romans 10:13 says, "Everyone who calls on the name of the Lord will be saved." That means no one is left out. Whether you feel broken, tired, or unsure, God is ready to receive you. His invitation is for all—young and old, rich and poor, strong and weak. Jesus came to help the hurting, not to judge them. He reached out to people others ignored. His love crosses every border and breaks every wall.

When you call on God, you are not bothering Him—you are blessing His heart. He delights in hearing your voice. He listens with love, responds with grace, and welcomes you with open arms. You don't need fancy words or perfect prayers. A simple cry from the heart is enough. God is not far away—He is near and ready. His invitation is not temporary—it's eternal. He doesn't just tolerate you—He treasures you.

You are not forgotten. God has not turned away from you. You are seen, known, and loved. No matter how far you feel, He is close. When you talk to Him, He listens. That moment begins a friendship filled with peace and purpose. His love brings comfort. His grace gives you a fresh start. His call invites you to something greater. Say yes to His love. Say yes to the new life He offers. He is waiting with open arms.

SYAVIHA MULENGYA

2. Cleansing

Many people carry guilt and shame from their past. They feel dirty inside and think God is angry with them. But God is full of mercy. **Hebrews 4:16** says, *"Let us come boldly to the throne of grace."* You don't have to hide—you can come close. Jesus forgave people who made big mistakes. He didn't push them away—He pulled them in. God doesn't wait for you to be perfect. He wants you just as you are.

Fear turns into faith when you trust God's love. Shame turns into strength when you receive His grace. God doesn't point fingers—He opens His arms. His mercy is fresh every morning. His love is stronger than your guilt. When you call on Him, He gives you a new beginning. You are not condemned—you are loved. You are not rejected—you are restored. God's cleansing is complete. He doesn't just wash the outside—He heals the heart. He removes the weight of sin and replaces it with peace. You don't have to carry your past anymore. You can walk in freedom. You can live with joy. You can stand with confidence. God's grace is greater than your mistakes. Call on Him and be made new.

3. Commitment

God wants to talk with you. He is not far away—He is close and caring. **James 4:8** says, *"Come near to God and He will come near to you."* Prayer is not about fancy words—it's about being honest. You can tell God your fears, your dreams, and your questions. He listens with love. When you speak, He hears. When you cry, He comforts. When you ask, He answers. Prayer fosters a deep and strong relationship with God. It brings peace to your heart and strength to your soul. You don't need to be perfect—just open. God is waiting for your voice. Talk to Him today. He's ready to walk with you.

SYAVIHA MULENGYA

4. Connection

God loves every person, every culture, and every language. **Revelation 7:9** shows people from all nations worshiping together in heaven. That is God's plan. Jesus didn't only stay with His own people—He reached out to others. He spoke to the Samaritan woman and healed the Roman officer's servant. His love has no borders. You are not a stranger to God—you are family. Whether you are new to a country or feel out of place, God sees you. He welcomes you. When you call on Him, you connect to a bigger story. You become part of a global family. In Christ, we are united. We celebrate our differences and share one faith.

5. Character

Who are you? The world may call you weak, broken, or forgotten. But God calls you strong, chosen, and loved. **2 Corinthians 5:17** says, *"If anyone is in Christ, he is a new creation."* That means your past does not define you. When you call on God, He gives you a new name and a new purpose. You are His child. You are valuable. You are called to do great things. God's truth replaces every lie. His love gives you confidence. You don't have to pretend—you can be who He made you to be. Your identity in Christ brings peace and power. You are not what others say—you are who God says.

6. Conversion

Sometimes we feel far from God. Life gets heavy. We make mistakes, and shame begins to whisper that we're no longer worthy. But God's love is stronger than our failures. **Isaiah 59:1** reminds us, *"Surely the arm of the Lord is not too short to save."* That means no matter how far we've wandered, He can still reach us. God doesn't turn away from broken people—He runs toward them. Repentance is not about fear or punishment; it's about returning to the One who loves us most. When we say, "God, I need You," He doesn't hesitate. He draws near, ready to forgive, heal, and restore. His grace meets us in our lowest place and lifts us higher than we ever imagined.

You don't have to stay stuck in guilt or regret. God offers a fresh start. He removes the things that block your heart—pain, pride, fear—and replaces them with peace, hope, and strength. Change doesn't happen all at once, but it begins with one call, one prayer, one step. That's how renewal begins. You are not too far gone. You are not forgotten. God is ready to rebuild your life, piece by piece, day by day. All He needs is your yes. When you call on Him, you step into a new story—one filled with grace, growth, and purpose.

7. Community

God's love is for everyone—not just a few. **John 3:16** says, *"God so loved the world."* That means every person matters. Jesus welcomed the poor, the sick, and the rejected. He broke rules to show love. Calling on God is not about joining a group—it's about knowing Him. You don't need a title—you need a heart that seeks Him. In God's family, there is room for all. No one is better than another. We are all saved by grace. When you call on God, you join a community of kindness, not competition. You are accepted. You are celebrated. You belong.

8. Calling

Many people wonder why they're here. They feel lost or unsure. But **Jeremiah 29:11** says, *"I know the plans I have for you,"* says the Lord. God made you for a reason. When you pray, He shows you your purpose. He reveals your gifts. He gives you courage. You don't have to guess—He will guide you. Calling on God brings clarity.

SYAVIHA MULENGYA

You start to see your path. You begin to walk with confidence. God doesn't make mistakes—He makes masterpieces. You are here to make a difference. Your life matters. Your voice matters.

9. Compassion

Guilt can feel heavy. It makes you feel stuck. But God's grace is stronger. **John 3:17** says, *"God did not send His Son to condemn the world, but to save it."* That means He wants to lift you, not crush you. Conviction helps you grow. Condemnation keeps you down. God corrects with love. He doesn't shame—He shapes. When you call on Him, He forgives. He gives you a clean heart. He replaces guilt with peace. Grace doesn't ignore your past—it heals it. You are not your mistakes. You are God's masterpiece.

10. Comfort

Life brings challenges. Pain can feel overwhelming, and loss leaves deep wounds. Yet in those moments, God is near. **Psalm 34:18** says, *"The Lord is close to the brokenhearted."* He doesn't turn away from sorrow—He draws near to it. Your tears matter to Him. Your cries are heard. You don't need to be strong to come to God; you just need to be honest. He welcomes everyone—no matter their background, mistakes, or struggles. His love reaches the hurting, the weary, and the forgotten. All who call on Him are received with open arms.

When you come to God, He doesn't just listen—He acts. He forgives what you regret, heals what's hurting, and begins to rebuild what's been broken. His peace calms anxious hearts. His strength lifts those who feel weak. He walks beside you through every storm, offering comfort and direction. God is not distant or silent—He is present and powerful. He restores what was lost and renews what feels worn out. You don't have to fix yourself first. Just come, and He will do the rest.

God also rewards those who trust Him. He replaces sorrow with joy, ashes with beauty, and confusion with purpose. He renews your strength day by day. Even in the darkest valley, He shines light on your path. Faith in Him is never wasted. He turns pain into testimony and trials into triumph. You are not alone. You are not forgotten. When you call on God, He receives you, restores your heart, renews your spirit, and rewards your faith.

SYAVIHA MULENGYA

1

BROKEN BUT YOU ARE HIS BEST

*****

The Hug That Heals — **Love That Lifts the Lost**

There are moments in life that change everything. Not through a loud sermon. Not through a miracle. But through something quiet, warm, and unexpected—like a hug.

It was a cold evening. Rain poured from the sky. The ground outside was full of mud. I had come to visit and pray in a home where the wife was waiting with hope. While we were praying, I heard the door open. Suddenly, the husband walked in. He didn't walk in proudly. He didn't walk in with strength. He came in slowly, almost falling with each step.

- His clothes were wet and covered in mud.

- His shoes left water prints on the floor.

- He smelled strongly of alcohol and sweat.

- His face looked tired, lost, and full of pain.

- His body was shaking and unsteady, and he had trouble walking.

SYAVIHA MULENGYA

It was clear he had fallen many times before entering the house. He looked confused, ashamed, and weak. He didn't speak. He just stood there, almost frozen.

His wife turned to me and whispered, "Man of God... don't hug him. He is dirty. He smells bad."

But when I saw him, I didn't see a drunk man. I saw someone who needed love. I felt the voice of God speak in my heart: **"He needs your embrace. He needs My love."**

So I walked up to him and hugged him tightly. The rain didn't matter. The smell didn't matter. The mud didn't matter.

He was shocked.

I held him and said in Swahili, **"Wewe ni mtu wa maana."** "You are a very important person."

He looked at me with tears and replied, "No, I'm not. I'm useless. That's what my wife calls me. She doesn't even give me food when I'm drunk."

I said again, "You are valuable. You are loved

Love: The Power That Breaks Chains

Love is the strongest force we have. It doesn't push away—it pulls people in. Love breaks down walls of pain, shame, and fear. When someone feels rejected by the world, your love can restore their worth. A simple hug, kind word, or smile can reach where long sermons cannot. That is what Jesus did—He loved people before correcting them. *"Above all, love each other deeply, because love covers over a multitude of sins."* (**1 Peter 4:8**)

God's love is unconditional. We are called to love others the same way. That means we don't wait until they are "cleaned up"—

we love them while they're in the mud. Love doesn't keep records; it builds bridges. When you show love to someone who feels lost, you become the hands of Jesus on earth. *"Let us not love with words or speech but with actions and in truth."* (**1 John 3:18**)

Listen: The Doorway to Healing

Listening is more than hearing—it's feeling. Many people in pain won't admit it. They will say, "I'm fine," even when they're drowning inside. When we listen with our hearts, not just our ears, we can hear the silent cries. Jesus listened to people that others ignored—He paid attention to the blind, the poor, the rejected. *"Everyone should be quick to listen, slow to speak and slow to become angry."* (**James 1:19**)

True listening brings comfort. It tells people, "You matter. Your voice is important." When someone knows they've been heard, healing begins. You don't need perfect words—just a caring heart. Be ready to listen, even when you don't understand everything. *"Carry each other's burdens, and in this way you will fulfill the law of Christ."* (**Galatians 6:2**)

Lift: Don't Look Down—Lift Up

Many people who are lost are not lazy—they're wounded. They've been pushed down, forgotten, or called worthless. God did not send us to look down on them, but to lift them up. Even a gentle word like "You are loved" can lift a soul that's been crushed. *"Therefore encourage one another and build each other up."* (**1 Thessalonians 5:11**)

Jesus lifted the woman caught in adultery, the thief on the cross, and the tax collector hiding in a tree. He lifted lives—so should we. Don't focus on the dirt they carry. Focus on the destiny God placed inside them. You may be the voice that reminds them of their value. *"The Lord upholds all who fall and lifts up all who are bowed down."* (**Psalm 145:14**)

Lead: Kindness That Points to Christ

To lead doesn't mean to control—it means to guide. And the best way to lead is through kindness. Jesus did not lead with condemnation; He led with compassion. He healed the broken, welcomed sinners, and shared meals with outcasts. *"Your kindness will lead us to repentance."* (**Romans 2:4, paraphrased**)

When people see kindness in you, they see a glimpse of God. You don't have to shout to lead—you can whisper truth and walk beside someone. Lead by example, not judgment. Speak life. Shine light. Hold hands through the dark until they see Jesus. *"Let your light shine before others, that they may see your good deeds and glorify your Father in heaven."* (**Matthew 5:16**).

God's Welcome Is Open to Everyone. "All Who Come Are Welcome" is a powerful truth from the heart of God. No one is too broken, too far gone, or too dirty to be embraced by His grace. Jesus never turned people away—He welcomed sinners, the sick, and the outcasts. God doesn't ask for a perfect past; He simply invites us to come. If you are tired, confused, hurting, or hungry for hope, you are invited. His arms are wide open, full of peace and love. *"Whoever comes to me I will never cast out."* (**John 6:37**). That means you. That means everyone. His welcome is warm, real, and waiting.

God Sees Potential, Not a Police Report

In the USA and many parts of the world, background checks often define your opportunities. If your history includes failure, sin, or setbacks, some doors may slam shut. But God's kingdom operates on a higher principle: mercy over memory. He doesn't examine your résumé for regrets—He examines your heart for readiness. People may judge, reject, or label you. But God sees beyond the broken pieces. He sees the masterpiece in the making. *"If anyone is in Christ, he is a new creation."* (**2 Corinthians 5:17**) Your past may be written in ink, but with God, the future is drafted in grace.

You may feel the sting of judgment—on paper, in interviews, or even in conversation. But God never defines you by your failures. He forgives the fallen, restores the ruined, and rebuilds the rejected. The cross is not a courtroom—it's a construction site. When others blacklist you, God bookmarks you. He doesn't consult your criminal record—He rewrites your character. God doesn't cancel your calling due to your past; He confirms it in spite of it. You are not a prisoner of who you were—you are being prepared for who you're becoming.

Come to Jesus and begin again. In His kingdom, there's no rejection—only redemption. He doesn't see a felon; He sees a future. No interview, fingerprint scan, or background check can erase the blood He shed for you. He receives the humbled, embraces the hurting, and empowers the hopeful. Your pain isn't the period—it's the comma before your comeback. Your record might intimidate people, but it inspires God to restore. Today is not too late. Grace is calling. Come as you are—He'll renew, redeem, and release you into your divine destiny.

God sees your worth, not weakness

When people look at you, they often see your mistakes first. They may notice your flaws, failures, or past sins. But God sees something else—He sees value. You may feel ashamed, broken, or stuck in a life that feels useless. But to God, you are not trash—you are treasure. He calls you wonderful, a winner, wise, and worthy.

He doesn't see your scars as shameful; He sees them as signs of survival. *"You are precious in my sight... and I love you."* (**Isaiah 43:4**)

Even when you don't believe in yourself, God does. He sees the beauty beneath your battles, the strength within your story, and the greatness underneath your grief. God doesn't measure you by your past—He looks at your potential. You are not forgotten—you are favored. You are not disqualified—you are deeply loved. Remember the man who came in drunk and dirty? Others saw filth. But God saw a future. His love lifted that man from the ground to grace. That same love is ready to lift you, too.

Come As You Are—He Will Change You

Many people think they must clean themselves up before they can come to God. They believe they need to be perfect, holy, and pure before they pray. But that's not what the Bible teaches. Jesus says clearly, *"Come now, and I will give you rest."* You don't need to wear a mask. You don't need to hide your pain or fix your problems before coming. God wants the real you. He invites you just as you are—broken, bruised, and burdened—and promises to heal you.

Think of the prodigal son. He walked home dirty, ashamed, and afraid. But his father didn't reject him—he ran, hugged him, and restored him. That's how God welcomes you. *"Let the one who is thirsty come and drink freely."* (**Revelation 22:17**) God doesn't wait for your perfection—He starts with your pain. He will receive you, renew your soul, reveal your purpose, and reward your faith. When you come to Him, your brokenness becomes a doorway. The moment you say yes, He begins a miracle inside of you. Come as you are. He will do the rest.

SYAVIHA MULENGYA

You Are a Miracle in the Making, Chosen, Not Forgotten

God doesn't call you a mistake—He calls you chosen. While others might reject you or remind you of your flaws, God declares, *"You are mine."* You may have been labeled, abandoned, or overlooked, but in His eyes, you are royalty. He made you on purpose, with a purpose, for great things. You are not a random creation—you are a divine design. He placed value in your soul and vision in your future. *"I have plans to give you hope and a future."* (**Jeremiah 29:11**). That's not just scripture—it's your story waiting to unfold.

You're not just surviving—you've been sent. You're not just alive—you are appointed. Despite the pain you've endured or the problems you've faced, God hasn't changed His mind about you. Your past does not cancel your calling. God uses the broken to bring breakthrough, and the hurting to bring healing. You may feel unqualified, but God qualifies the willing. He gives grace to those who are ready to receive it. In Him, your identity is restored, your value revealed, and your future redeemed.

In God's kingdom, all who come are welcome. No paperwork, no prerequisites, no rejection. Just love, grace, and open arms. Whether you're wounded, weary, or wondering why, there's a seat for you. You're not only invited—you're expected. God stands at the door of your heart, not with judgment but with joy. He offers peace for your pain, healing for your hurt, and purpose for your path. This message matters—because someone needs to know: it's never too late, and you're never too lost. Transformation is waiting. Just come.

2

WHERE ARE YOU, MY DEAR ONE

*****

A mother sent her son overseas for higher studies, proud and hopeful. One day, the son's phone malfunctioned. When he finally turned it on, he was shocked—over twenty missed calls from his mom. She hadn't just waited quietly; she had called the apartment, tried reaching his friends, and even contacted the police out of concern. The mother was on the edge of booking a flight just to find him. Why? Because he was her treasure. Her laughter over the call wasn't mockery—it was relief. She would do *anything* to reach him. That's the heartbeat of God.

God is like that mother. He has been calling—day after day, moment after moment—not just once, but over and over. Through His Word, His Spirit, sermons, songs, and even silent moments, He's whispering: *"Come back to Me. I love you."* He's not angry. He's aching to reconnect. When we ignore Him, get lost in busyness, or feel too broken to answer, He doesn't give up. Every missed call from heaven is a message of mercy. God isn't just reaching for you—He's running after you.

SYAVIHA MULENGYA

The son's question—"Why did you call so many times?"—was met with a mother's laughter and love: *"You're my treasure. I would do anything to find you."* That's how God sees you. No mistake, pain, or distance can make Him forget you. You are dear to Him. He doesn't call to condemn—He calls to connect. He's ready to cross oceans of doubt and fear just to reach your heart. You matter to God more than you can imagine. When others let go, He still holds on.

God calls every day. He calls the hurting, the hopeful, the hidden, and the hardened. He calls not with judgment, but with joy. When you finally answer, He doesn't scold—He celebrates. Like the prodigal son's father, He'll run to embrace you. The missed calls aren't guilt—they're grace. This isn't just a story—it's a summons. God is calling you now. Not to shame you, but to save you. Don't let today be another missed moment. Pick up the call. Come as you are. There's love, healing, and home waiting for you.

Just as the mother kept calling her son more than twenty times when she couldn't reach him—willing even to fly across countries just to find him—God is calling you every day because you are His treasure. Her words, *"You are dear to me, I would do everything to look for you,"* mirror the voice of heaven that cries out, *"I have loved you with an everlasting love"* (**Jeremiah 31:3**). God doesn't abandon the unreachable; He relentlessly pursues the lost, reaching through silence, struggle, and shame just to restore relationship. *"Here I am! I stand at the door and knock. If anyone hears My voice and opens the door, I will come in…"* (**Revelation 3:20**). His calls aren't random—they are filled with purpose and compassion. You are not forgotten. You are being found.

SYAVIHA MULENGYA

1. Hear You

God is calling to hear you, because your voice matters in heaven. He hears your pain, your praise, your prayers, and your potential. Even when others ignore you, He inclines His ear toward you. *"The righteous cry out, and the Lord hears them."* (**Psalm 34:17**) You're not just making noise—you're making contact with the Creator.

God calls to hear your desires, your doubts, and your dreams. He listens when you're joyful and when you're broken. His presence is personal. He's not just recording your words—He's responding with love. What touches your heart touches His.

Every time you speak to God, you're entering a divine conversation. You're not a stranger—you're His child. In calling you, God is saying: *"Talk to Me. Trust Me. Tell Me."* Heaven is listening, and your words have weight in the courts of glory.

2. Help You

God calls you because He's ready to help. His help is holy, healing, and hands-on. He doesn't just watch from afar—He steps in. When you're weak, He becomes your strength. When you're lost, He becomes your guide. *"Fear not, I am with you… I will help you."* (**Isaiah 41:10**)

Help from God brings peace to your problems, answers to your confusion, and power to your purpose. He doesn't just patch wounds—He gives wisdom. He supplies what you lack and multiplies what you offer. His help covers the past, empowers the present, and prepares the future.

God's help makes your journey possible. With Him, mountains move, doors open, and hope rises. He's calling because He's committed—not just to saving you, but to sustaining you. When heaven helps, no opposition can hinder.

3. Honor You

You are not an accident—you are anointed. God is calling you because He wants to honor you, not for what the world says you've earned, but for who He says you are. You're not forgotten—you're favored. He chooses you before you're noticed, blesses you before you're praised, and calls you His own long before the crowd approves. *"You are precious and honored in My sight, and I love you."* (**Isaiah 43:4**) This is not about pride—it's about purpose. You are a divine masterpiece marked with heavenly significance. God doesn't wait for man's permission to lift you—He acts on His promises.

His honor doesn't just give titles—it gives transformation. He lifts you out of shame and places you in strength. He replaces rejection with recognition, sorrow with celebration, and ashes with beauty. You may feel broken, but God calls you beloved. His honor is healing and elevating. It restores your dignity, renews your confidence, and revives your destiny. He doesn't just forgive you— He favors you. He doesn't just accept you—He affirms you. God's honor is not occasional; it's eternal.

Honor from God also carries responsibility. He entrusts you with influence—not to inflate your ego, but to impact lives. When God honors you, He sets you apart to speak truth, serve others, and shine with His glory. You're not called to compete—you're called to contribute. He positions you for divine impact. Answering His call is stepping boldly into your identity as a vessel of purpose, wrapped in grace, rooted in humility, and clothed in spiritual authority. You are honored to honor Him back.

SYAVIHA MULENGYA

4. Hide You

God calls to hide you—not to isolate you, but to insulate you. The hidden place is where you're sheltered, shaped, and secured. *"He will hide me in His shelter…"* (**Psalm 27:5**). In hiding, God is preserving you from harm and preparing you for harvest.

Sometimes, God hides you to protect your peace from the pressure of others. He shields you from attacks, distractions, and deception. In the secret place, you find intimacy with Him, identity in Him, and instruction from Him. It's not rejection—it's redirection.

Being hidden doesn't mean forgotten—it means refined. Like gold in the furnace, your faith grows strong in silence. God's hiding is holy. You're not buried—you're being built. Trust the process. When the time is right, He will reveal what He has healed.

5. Harness You

God is calling you to harness your gifts. You are loaded with potential, filled with fire, and chosen for change. His call activates what's dormant and directs it toward destiny. *"We have different gifts according to the grace given to each of us."* (**Romans 12:6**).

To harness is to focus, channel, and release. Your talents are not for waste—they're for warfare. Your story carries healing. Your voice carries vision. Your journey carries answers for someone else. He harnesses you to build His kingdom and bless His people.

God sharpens you through His Spirit and strengthens you through His Word. You are not random—you are a resource. His call is your command to rise. When heaven harnesses your life, you become a messenger of hope, healing, and harmony.

SYAVIHA MULENGYA

6. Heal You

Finally, God is calling to heal you, not with temporary relief, but with lasting restoration. His healing is not just for your body, but for your soul, your memories, your identity. It's not just a moment—it's a movement. God reaches into the deepest wounds and touches the places no one else sees. *"He heals the brokenhearted and binds up their wounds."* (**Psalm 147:3**) His healing is gentle but powerful. He doesn't rush the process; He walks with you through it. Every scar tells a story, but in His hands, that story becomes strength.

He heals your past with His mercy, washing away guilt and regret. He silences shame with forgiveness and fills broken gaps with grace. Then He brings peace to your present—calming storms in your mind, softening bitterness in your heart, and restoring clarity to your steps. And He heals your future with purpose. You're not defined by what hurt you—you're refined by what He's doing in you. No sin is too dark, no situation too hopeless, no soul too shattered. When God heals, He doesn't patch—He transforms. He restores your joy, renews your mind, and resurrects your destiny.

When you receive His healing, you rise stronger. Healing makes you whole—but it also makes you a witness. You no longer just survive; you shine. Your pain becomes a platform. Your scars speak of victory, not defeat. God's healing is more than personal—it's powerful enough to overflow. You become a channel of comfort, a carrier of courage, a testimony of transformation. His call to heal is a call to launch—to step into bold faith, radiant freedom, and purposeful greatness. When He heals you, He prepares you for a life that blesses others and glorifies Him.

When God calls you, **just answer,** no hesitation, no fear. You don't need to understand everything or have it all figured out. His

SYAVIHA MULENGYA

call is not based on your qualifications, but on His compassion. Don't worry about your weaknesses, He equips whom He calls. You're not stepping out alone; you're stepping with the One who walks on water and calms every storm. When God speaks, it's not just a suggestion—it's a summons into something greater.

Do not ask yourself a thousand questions. Faith doesn't begin with answers—it begins with obedience. When God says *"Go,"* your "Yes" opens the door to growth, greatness, and grace. People may doubt you, criticize you, or even discourage you. But their words don't define your walk. The voice of God is louder than the voices of fear. He doesn't call the perfect—He perfects those He calls. So let go of overthinking. Trust His timing, His leading, and His love.

And above all, **do not feel ashamed.** God is not pointing at your past—He's pointing to your purpose. Shame says, "You're not worthy"—but grace says, "You're chosen." The One who calls you is the One who cleanses you, covers you, and crowns you. Lift your head. Stand in your calling. Let the world see the beauty of someone who dared to obey heaven. Because when God says *"I am here,"* He means you are never alone—you are deeply loved, divinely called, and destined to shine.

God Is Your Safety. When life feels heavy and hard, God is still with you. Even when no one picks up the phone or answers your cry, He is near. When your heart is hurting, He holds it with care. When you feel alone, He stays close and never leaves your side.

You can talk to God anytime—morning, night, or in the middle of your pain. He listens when others don't. He understands what you can't explain. He doesn't judge your tears or your silence. He welcomes you just as you are, with love and grace.

SYAVIHA MULENGYA

Psalm 46:1 says, "God is our refuge and strength, a very present help in trouble." That means He is your safe place, your shelter, and your steady rock. When everything around you feels shaky, He remains strong. You can trust Him to carry you through.

God Is Your Strength. When you feel weak, tired, or worried, God is still with you. He gives strength when you have none left. If you fall again and again, He helps you get back up. When you feel stuck, He helps you move forward. The Bible says, *"He gives power to the weak and strength to the powerless"* (Isaiah 40:29). God doesn't blame you for your mistakes—He wants to heal them. He doesn't ignore your pain—He carries it with you. He doesn't leave when things get hard—He stays close. Broken things can be fixed. Lost hope can be found again. What was torn down can be rebuilt. Dry hearts can be filled with joy. God is your strength, your helper, and your hope.

God Is Your Source. When the road is rough and the way is unclear, God is your God. His Word lights your path like a lamp in the dark. His voice speaks peace when the world shouts fear. His Spirit leads you with love and wisdom. **Psalm 34:18** says, *"The Lord is close to the brokenhearted and saves those who are crushed in spirit."* He knows your thoughts, your dreams, your doubts. He loves you deeply, even when you feel unlovable. He draws near when you feel far away. He doesn't flinch at your flaws. He doesn't reject your realness. You can tell Him everything—your joy, your pain, your questions. You can trust Him to guide you, guard you, and grow you. He is your God—always faithful, always present, always good.

3

YOU ARE SO PRECIOUS

*****

There comes a sacred moment in every life when heaven reaches out. It doesn't shout, but it speaks clearly. God's voice breaks through fear, noise, and confusion and gently calls you by name. This is not just another day—it's a divine invitation to change your direction, deepen your walk, and discover your worth. God's call isn't about religion—it's about relationship. It's the moment where your past no longer holds you, and your future begins to unfold. Answering His call is stepping out of fear and into favor. It's where survival ends and significance begins. It's the doorway to a new beginning shaped by grace and filled with purpose.

You may question your value. You may ask, "Why would God choose someone like me?" But heaven always has an answer: "Because I created you, I love you, and I have a plan for you." God doesn't wait for perfect conditions—He meets you where you are and walks with you as you grow. When you say "Yes" to Him, the impossible becomes possible. His power strengthens your steps, and His peace surrounds your heart. Saying "Yes" releases divine

SYAVIHA MULENGYA

strategy, supernatural strength, and God's guidance for every challenge ahead.

That "Yes" unlocks four incredible blessings in your life. First, you begin to **Receive** heaven's peace, provision, and presence. Then, God begins to **Restore** what was broken—your joy, your calling, your confidence. Third, He starts to **Reveal** what's been hidden—your identity, your gifts, your mission. And finally, you walk into your **Reward**—a life of fulfillment, favor, and eternal impact. These are not temporary changes—they are lasting shifts that align you with God's purpose and equip you for every season.

The truth is this: God is not looking for the perfect; He's calling the willing. You don't have to understand everything; you just need to trust the One who does. His love is patient. His call is powerful. His timing is perfect. When you answer, you walk into a life you were always meant to live. Don't hesitate. Don't let doubt delay your destiny. This is your moment—your invitation to rise, to shine, and to become all God created you to be. Just say "Yes.

1. Receive: You Receive Heaven's Presence, Provision, Power, and Peace

When you answer God's call, you are not simply stepping into a new season—you are stepping under a supernatural covering. You receive immediate access to His presence, which fills the room with peace and wraps your spirit in strength. You are welcomed, not tolerated. You are invited, not ignored. *"Come near to God and He will come near to you."* (**James 4:8**). That closeness becomes your confidence. You're no longer stumbling alone—you're walking under open heavens where miracles move and favor flows.

His call comes with promises—both written and whispered. What He has spoken over your life cannot be canceled, even by your past or your pain. You begin to receive assurance, direction, and divine strategy. *"For all the promises of God in Him are Yes, and in Him Amen."* (**2 Corinthians 1:20**). Every time you say "Yes" to God, He opens another window from heaven to release what's already been prepared. Faith unlocks it. Obedience activates it.

You also receive supernatural provision. Where there was a lack, there is now a supply. Where you once worried about how— it becomes clear Who. God becomes your provider, your sustainer, your source. *"My God will supply every need of yours according to His riches in glory."* (**Philippians 4:19**) The provision touches every area—spiritual, emotional, physical, and financial. You may start with nothing, but with God, you lack nothing.

And perhaps the greatest gift you receive is His unfailing love. When you answer His call, you stop chasing approval and start living accepted. His love quiets your shame, lifts your head, and fills every void. *"I have loved you with an everlasting love."* (**Jeremiah 31:3**). You're not just covered—you're carried. You don't just walk with blessings—they begin to follow you everywhere. *"Surely goodness and mercy shall follow me all the days of my life."* (**Psalm 23:6**).

2. Restore: You Are Renewed in Every Area of Life

When you answer God's call, He doesn't just take you back— He brings you forward, renewed. Restoration begins from the inside out. He heals the hidden places, untangles the confusion, and replaces weariness with wonder. *"He restores my soul; He leads me in paths of righteousness."* (**Psalm 23:3**). His restoration isn't cosmetic—it's transformational. It touches your thoughts, emotions, and identity in ways you couldn't even describe.

God restores your confidence so you can stand tall. He restores your courage so you can move forward with faith. He restores your calling, bringing clarity to what you're created to do. The pain that tried to paralyze you now becomes proof of God's power. *"Instead of your shame you will receive a double portion... everlasting joy will be yours."* (**Isaiah 61:7**). What tried to break you now builds you. Restoration turns your mess into a ministry.

Relationships that were strained by past wounds begin to mend. God restores connection, compassion, and communication, not just with people, but with Himself as well. You feel spiritually alive again. Vision that was blurry becomes vivid. Energy that felt lost begins to overflow. *"I will repay you for the years the locusts have eaten."* (**Joel 2:25**). Nothing is wasted when God restores. Even lost time becomes redeemed time.

And most importantly, God restores your identity. He removes labels, lies, and limitations. You stop living as a victim and start walking in victory. You're not just forgiven—you're commissioned. *"You will be called by a new name that the mouth of the Lord will bestow."* (**Isaiah 62:2**). When restoration flows, shame flees, and you begin living like the masterpiece you truly are.

3. Reveal: God Unfolds Your True Identity, Assignment, and Destiny

When you answer God's call, something sacred begins to unfold: He starts revealing who you truly are—not what the world calls you, but what heaven named you. You are not average or overlooked—you are anointed. *"Before I formed you in the womb I knew you, before you were born I set you apart."* (**Jeremiah 1:5**). Your identity becomes clearer. You're not just living—you're called. You're not just existing—you're appointed for impact.

He reveals your assignment—the people you're called to reach, the problems you're created to solve, the places you're destined to influence. Clarity replaces confusion. Suddenly, your gifts make sense, your story gains direction, and your passion finds a purpose. *"The purposes of a person's heart are deep waters, but one who has insight draws them out."* (**Proverbs 20:5**). God draws out the depth within you that even you didn't see.

As you walk with God, layers of fear and doubt begin to lift, and fresh wisdom settles in your spirit. You stop chasing trends and start embracing truth. His Word becomes a lamp, lighting steps you never dared to take. *"Your word is a lamp to my feet and a light to my path."* (**Psalm 119:105**). He doesn't just reveal what to do—He reveals why it matters.

And He reveals your destiny—not a vague dream, but a divine design. You begin to understand your role in the bigger story of grace and glory. Every detail of your life is threaded with purpose. You're not random—you're royal. God's call reveals your future, your influence, and your eternal value. *"What no eye has seen, what no ear has heard… these are the things God has revealed to us by His Spirit."* (**1 Corinthians 2:9-10**).

4. Reward: You Step into Divine Favor, Fulfillment, and Eternal Impact

When you answer God's call, you step into a reward that is rich, real, and lasting. God does not forget faithfulness. His reward is both personal and purposeful. *"God is not unjust; He will not forget your work and the love you have shown Him."* (**Hebrews 6:10**). You begin to experience favor that you didn't earn—grace that opens doors, peace that surpasses understanding, and joy that rises even in trials. Your obedience becomes the key to unlocked blessings.

The reward includes fulfillment—your soul finds satisfaction not in success alone, but in significance. You realize your life matters.

Every act of service, every word of encouragement, every step of surrender brings fruit. *"Well done, good and faithful servant! You have been faithful with a few things; I will put you in charge of many."* (**Matthew 25:21**). God rewards faithfulness with more opportunity, more influence, and more revelation.

Your reward also becomes visible through legacy. What you do now begins to outlive you. Others are changed because you answered the call. Your story becomes someone's survival guide. *"Those who are wise will shine like the brightness of the heavens, and those who lead many to righteousness, like the stars forever and ever."* (**Daniel 12:3**). You don't just make waves—you ignite movements.

And finally, the greatest reward is intimacy with God Himself. You walk with Him not just as Creator, but as Companion. His presence becomes your portion, and His voice becomes your victory. You're not just building earthly success—you're storing eternal treasure. *"Blessed is the one who perseveres under trial because, having stood the test, that person will receive the crown of life."* (**James 1:12**). The reward of obedience reaches beyond this life—into eternity.

4

ALL ARE WELCOME

*****

1. Come As You Are

God's invitation is simple, sincere, and supernatural: "Come." He doesn't ask you to clean yourself up before approaching Him. He doesn't demand perfection, performance, or pedigree. He simply says, "Come as you are." Whether you are broken, burdened, bruised, or battling guilt, you are welcome. His love is not based on your condition—it's based on His compassion. He sees your heart, hears your cry, and welcomes your presence. As Jesus said, *"Come to me, all you who are weary and burdened, and I will give you rest"* (**Matthew 11:28 NIV**).

Many people feel they must hide their pain or pretend to be someone they're not. They wear smiles that mask sorrow and silence that hides shame. But God sees beyond the surface. He knows the real you—the one behind the mask, behind the mistakes, behind the memories. And still, He loves you. He doesn't shame you for your past; He saves you for your future. He doesn't expose your flaws; He embraces your faith. *"The Lord looks at the heart"* (**1 Samuel 16:7**), and what He sees is someone worth redeeming.

SYAVIHA MULENGYA

When you share your story with people, they may judge, reject, or remind you of your failures. But when you share it with Christ, He covers it with grace. He doesn't keep a record of wrongs—He rewrites your record with righteousness. He doesn't remind you of your sins—He removes them. *"If anyone is in Christ, the new creation has come: The old has gone, the new is here!"* (**2 Corinthians 5:17**). In His presence, you are not condemned; you are cleansed. You are not cast out; you are called in.

So come boldly. Come broken. Come believing. You are not too far gone. You are not too messed up. You are not forgotten. You are forgiven. All who come are welcome—not because of who they are, but because of who He is. His grace is greater than your guilt. His mercy is deeper than your mistakes. And His love is stronger than your shame. *"Whoever comes to me I will never drive away"* (**John 6:37**). That promise is for you—today, just as you are

God's Invitation Is a Promise

In God's Kingdom, *all* are welcome. This isn't just a kind phrase—it's an eternal promise. God doesn't wait for you to get everything right before He embraces you. He's not searching for perfect records, polished prayers, or flawless personalities. What He longs for is a surrendered heart. *"The sacrifices of God are a broken spirit; a broken and contrite heart, O God, you will not despise"* (**Psalm 51:17**).

No matter your past, your pain, or your personality, His invitation stands open. His arms are not closed to the wounded— they are wide open to the weary. *"Come, all you who are thirsty, come to the waters"* (**Isaiah 55:1**). This is not a temporary offer— it's a timeless truth.

You Are Not Too Broken to Belong

You might feel broken, burdened, boring, or beyond repair—but God sees value, beauty, and purpose in you. The world may overlook you, but heaven never does. The Bible declares, *"Whoever comes to Me I will never drive away"* (**John 6:37**). That means you're not just accepted—you're cherished.

In a world quick to reject, God chooses to receive. He doesn't just allow you in—He rejoices over you. *"The Lord your God is with you… He will take great delight in you; in His love He will no longer rebuke you, but will rejoice over you with singing"* (**Zephaniah 3:17**). You are not a problem to be fixed—you are a person to be loved.

Grace Breaks Every Barrier

God doesn't close doors on the struggling. He opens wide the gate of grace. While the world may label you, limit you, or leave you behind, God builds bridges to your heart. He looks past the external and sees what others miss. *"The Lord does not see as man sees; man looks at the outward appearance, but the Lord looks at the heart"* (**1 Samuel 16:7**).

His love reaches places judgment cannot. His mercy moves mountains that shame cannot climb. Grace is not earned—it's extended. And once received, it transforms everything it touches.

You Are Called Home

God knows your entire story—every chapter, every challenge, every choice—and still calls you His. He doesn't see failure; He sees family. He doesn't measure you by what you've done but by what He's destined you to become. *"See what great love the Father has lavished on us, that we should be called children of God!"* (**1 John 3:1**).

SYAVIHA MULENGYA

You were created to belong, not to be cast aside. And today, that door is still open, and your seat at His table is waiting. *"You prepare a table before me... surely goodness and mercy shall follow me all the days of my life, and I will dwell in the house of the Lord forever"* (**Psalm 23:5–6**).

Grace Breaks Every Barrier. God doesn't close doors on the struggling. He opens wide the gate of grace. While the world may label you, limit you, or leave you behind, God builds bridges to your heart. He looks past the external and sees what others miss. *"The Lord does not see as man sees; man looks at the outward appearance, but the Lord looks at the heart"* (**1 Samuel 16:7**). His love reaches places judgment cannot.

You Are Called Home. God knows your entire story—every chapter, every challenge, every choice—and still calls you *His*. He doesn't see failure; He sees family. He doesn't measure you by what you've done but by what He's destined you to become. You were created to belong, not to be cast aside. And today, that door is still open, and your seat at His table is waiting.

Many people walk through life believing lies that limit their identity, confidence, and joy. These lies often come wrapped in familiar voices, deep feelings, and painful memories—but none of them speak for God. In His Kingdom, everyone is welcome. You're not forgotten, rejected, or too far gone. You are loved, valued, and invited to rise above every label and limitation. Don't live below your worth—God calls you higher. So today is the moment to choose freedom.

Stop

1. **Listening to the wrong voice**

2. **Looking down on yourself**

SYAVIHA MULENGYA

3. **Living in fear and doubt**

4. **Lying to yourself**

5. **Losing hope**

1. Listening to the Wrong Voice

Let's be honest—life is noisy. There are voices from our past, from people around us, and even from within that whisper defeat, shame, and doubt. They say things like *"You'll never be enough"* or *"God has forgotten you."* But these are not God's words—they're lies meant to drain your strength. The Word says, *"My sheep hear My voice... and they follow Me"* (**John 10:27**). That means you can tune out the noise and tune in to truth.

God's voice is not loud with condemnation—it's gentle with compassion. He doesn't say, *"Get it all together,"* before welcoming you. He says, *"Come to Me, all who are weary..."* (**Matthew 11:28**). His invitation isn't selective—it's sacred and universal. You are wanted. You are called. You are welcome.

So today, let go of the noise that distracts you from your worth. Let go of the criticism that clouds your clarity. Choose to listen to the Shepherd who speaks life. *"There is now no condemnation for those who are in Christ Jesus"* (**Romans 8:1**). His voice leads you not into guilt—but into grace.

2. Looking Down on Yourself

You were never meant to live bowed by shame or insecurity. God created you in His image—beautiful, bold, and blessed. *"I praise You because I am fearfully and wonderfully made"* (**Psalm 139:14**). That means every part of you carries divine intention. The enemy wants you to forget your value, but God wants you to live with vision.

SYAVIHA MULENGYA

No matter who's walked away from you or what you've walked through, your identity hasn't changed. You are not second-class in God's Kingdom. You are not overlooked—you are over-loved. *"Even the very hairs of your head are all numbered"* (**Luke 12:7**). That's how carefully and completely God sees you.

Lift your eyes. Lift your heart. Lift your posture. You are not beneath—you've been seated with Christ in heavenly places (**Ephesians 2:6**). Don't allow lies to hold you down when love is calling you higher. God says you're qualified—and when God speaks, no one can revoke it.

3. Living in Fear and Doubt

Fear is a thief. It robs you of peace, joy, and progress. Doubt is a fog—it makes you question what God has already promised. But here's what Scripture says: *"God has not given us a spirit of fear, but of power, love, and a sound mind"* (**2 Timothy 1:7**). That means fear doesn't come from Him—and you don't have to live under it.

Faith doesn't mean you always feel brave—it means you believe beyond your feelings. Abraham didn't know where he was going, but he still moved. Peter stepped out of the boat in a storm—but he stepped toward Jesus. You don't need perfect conditions to walk by faith—you just need obedience.

So let go of fear. Break free from doubt. Trust the One who is faithful to complete what He started in you. *"Without faith it is impossible to please God..."* (**Hebrews 11:6**). You are welcome to live free—not afraid. Boldness is not only your calling—it's your covenant.

4. Lying to Yourself

We often say things in secret that sabotage our future. Lies like *"I'm not lovable," "I'll always be stuck,"* or *"God skipped me."* These statements don't reflect heaven's opinion—they reflect hurt. But God's Word stands above every lie. *"You will know the truth, and the truth will set you free"* (**John 8:32**). Truth speaks healing. Lies speak hindrance.

God sees you fully—and still loves you completely. He doesn't name you by your mistakes. He calls you by your destiny. *"If anyone is in Christ, he is a new creation. The old is gone, the new has come"* (**2 Corinthians 5:17**). That's not a metaphor—it's a miracle. You're not defined by defeat. You're designed for victory.

Speak life. Speak light. Speak liberty. Cancel the lies with the language of love. You are forgiven, favored, and free. Today is the day to rewrite the narrative—with God's truth at the center. Your story isn't over—it's just beginning.

5. Losing Hope

Hope isn't just a feeling—it's fuel. When we lose hope, we lose drive, direction, and determination. Life gets dark. Dreams fade. Despair grows. But God is the God of hope—not just in good times, but especially in hard times. *"May the God of hope fill you with all joy and peace as you trust in Him..."* (**Romans 15:13**).

The night may be long—but joy is promised at dawn. *"Weeping may endure for a night, but joy comes in the morning"* (**Psalm 30:5**). That's not just poetic—it's prophetic. Even in seasons of sorrow, hope is rising behind the curtain. God is working—even when you're waiting.

SYAVIHA MULENGYA

Don't give up. Don't give in. Don't stay stuck. Hope invites you to dream again. To believe again. To breathe again. Your tomorrow is not buried—it's being built. The King who called you will keep you. You are welcome to rise again. And this time, you're rising with hope in your hands.

5

RISE UP WHEN YOU FALL

*****

When You Fall, God Still Calls

Life is full of ups and downs, and no path is always smooth. Sometimes we walk on mountaintops with joy, peace, and a strong faith. Other times, we feel tired, broken, and confused in deep valleys. We fall into doubt, sin, sadness, or fear. But falling does not mean we are finished. It means we are human, still learning, and still growing. The Bible says, *"Though he falls, he shall not be utterly cast down..."* (**Psalm 37:24**). God holds our hand even when we stumble. His grace meets us in the valley and lifts us to victory. When we fall, God's love becomes our ladder to rise again.

God stays faithful, even when we are weak or faithless. He doesn't run away when we mess up—He comes closer. The Bible shows us the Father who welcomed the lost son with open arms. He forgives quickly, He finds us, He fights our battles. He walks with us through the storm and whispers peace in pain. Paul reminds us, *"If we are faithless, He remains faithful..."* (**2 Timothy 2:13**). We may lose our strength, but we never lose His support. God's love doesn't depend on your perfection—it responds to your honesty.

You may fall, but you will not fall alone. You are still loved, still wanted, still pursued.

Your brokenness can lead to your breakthrough. God doesn't throw away those who are hurting—He heals them. He takes your pain and makes something powerful from it. You are still useful, still chosen, still important. The Bible says, *"The righteous fall seven times and rise again"* (**Proverbs 24:16**). God shapes your life like clay in His hands. He rebuilds you with new strength, new joy, and new purpose. This message is not about guilt—it's about growth. It gives you a plan to rise again through eight simple steps. When you fall, you can rise. And when you rise, you rise with God

1. Admit the Fall

Admitting you've fallen is not weakness—it's wisdom. The truth sets you free, and honesty opens the door to healing. When David cried out, *"I have sinned against the Lord,"* he opened himself to God's restoration (**2 Samuel 12:13**). Stop hiding—start healing. Denial delays destiny, but truth invites transformation. You can't fix what you won't face, and you can't rise if you won't recognize you've stumbled. Grace begins where pride ends. Let your words be bold and broken: "Lord, I missed it." That confession becomes the first step to recovery. No more excuses—just embrace the truth and let healing begin.

Acknowledgment is not just for God—it's for your soul. When you name the mistake, you tame its shame. The devil wants you to be silent, but God invites you into the light. **Psalm 32:5** says, *"Then I acknowledged my sin... and You forgave."* The moment you acknowledge, Heaven responds with mercy. This is the power of truth—it breaks guilt's grip and welcomes God's grace. You're not condemned—you're being cleansed. Take off the mask and let the mercy flow. The fall is real, but so is the forgiveness. Stop minimizing the mistake and start maximizing God's mercy.

When you acknowledge the fall, you also awaken the fighter within. God doesn't leave you in the mud—He lifts you from it. The cry of the heart leads to the comfort of Heaven. Now your soul can start the climb. Like the prodigal son, coming to your senses begins with coming to truth. **Luke 15:18**—*"I will arise and go to my father."* That's where restoration begins. Don't fear the truth—face it, embrace it, and walk out of the shadows. Because when you acknowledge, God rebuilds. And this rebuilding brings a revival to your heart.

2 Access God's Grace

You can't earn grace—it's a gift freely given. When you feel unworthy, grace speaks worth. Hebrews 4:16 says, *"Come boldly to the throne of grace…"* That invitation is still open. Grace doesn't wait for perfection—it responds to honesty. No matter how deep the fall, grace reaches deeper. Jesus stretched His arms to cover your shame with love. You are not rejected—you are redeemed. This grace lifts your head and holds your heart. Stop running from God and start running to Him. The throne is not for judgment—it's for mercy.

Accessing grace means letting go of self-dependence. When you rely on your own strength, you carry the weight of guilt. But when you lean on God, you receive the power to rise again. Paul said, *"My grace is sufficient for you…"* (**2 Corinthians 12:9**). That means you lack nothing in God. Grace doesn't patch up your past— it rewrites your story. Come as you are—not as you think you should be. The pressure is off because grace is on. Let grace guide your steps, clean your slate, and strengthen your spirit. You're not just surviving—you're walking in supernatural strength.

SYAVIHA MULENGYA

Grace is not a one-time miracle—it's a daily lifeline. Like manna in the wilderness, God's grace is fresh each morning. **Lamentations 3:23** says, *"New every morning is Your mercy."* That means no expiration, no limitation, just restoration. Don't live on yesterday's grace—ask for more today. Prayer keeps you connected. Worship keeps you grounded. Scripture keeps you focused. Let grace cover your every moment, conversation, and decision. When you access grace, you access power—and that power transforms every fall into a future.

3. Accept God's Forgiveness

Forgiveness is God's healing medicine for the soul. But you must take it in to be changed by it. **Hebrews 8:12** says, *"I will remember their sins no more."* That's God's promise—not your feeling. Guilt says you're stuck—God says you're free. Shame whispers lies—God speaks life. You don't have to beg for mercy— it's already paid for. Jesus carried it all so you could carry peace. Accept forgiveness like a gift with your name on it. Don't argue with grace—agree with it.

Accepting forgiveness means living free from self-condemnation. **Psalm 103:12** declares, *"As far as the east is from the west…"*—that's how far your sin has been removed. God separates you from the stain so you can step into significance. Let the enemy's accusations fall flat. You're not who you were—you're becoming who God sees. Walk in confidence, not guilt. The blood of Jesus speaks louder than your mistake. Stop defining yourself by what you did—start declaring who God says you are. You are clean. You are new. You are free.

When forgiveness fills your heart, freedom follows your steps. The past loses its power. Your future gains momentum. You're not dragging the weight of failure—you're dancing with grace. **Romans**

8:1—*"There is now no condemnation…"* That's your anthem. Let go of the inner critic and grab hold of God's truth. Accept His forgiveness fully—not halfway. Let it reach the deepest place. Forgiveness is not weak—it's a weapon. It breaks every chain and builds a new chapter of victory.

4. Ask for Forgiveness

Healing starts with humility. Asking for forgiveness is not defeat—it's deliverance. **Matthew 5:24** says, *"Go and be reconciled…"* That means don't delay—repair the broken bridge. Pride postpones peace, but humility unlocks healing. Say, "I was wrong," and watch walls fall down. It's not about perfect words— it's about a pure heart. God honors the honest. Relationships mend when humility leads. Asking is hard—but healing is worth it.

Ask God boldly and sincerely. Don't come with fancy phrases— just come with truth. **Psalm 51:1** pleads, *"Have mercy on me, O God."* That's enough to move Heaven. When you confess, you're not just talking—you're transforming. **James 5:16** says, *"Confess… pray… be healed."* Repentance is not shameful—it's powerful. Ask with faith, not fear. God never turns away a repentant soul. The moment you ask, mercy meets you. The tears are seen. The pain is heard. And grace is released.

Asking others for forgiveness is healing, too. Don't run from the hard conversation—run into it with love. Reconciliation isn't weakness—it's wisdom. Your relationships matter to God. Forgiveness mends families, friendships, and faith communities. When you ask, you invite peace into the space where pain once lived. It won't always be easy—but it will always be sacred. Honor the one you wronged. Release the hurt. And let God restore what was broken.

SYAVIHA MULENGYA

5. Appreciate the Forgiveness

Gratitude is how you guard the gift of grace. When you've been forgiven, your soul sings a new song. **Luke 7:47** reminds us, *"She loved much because she was forgiven much."* That's the power of appreciation—it turns mercy into melody. Don't overlook the miracle of forgiveness. Let it soak into your spirit and shine through your speech. Say "Thank You, Lord" not just in prayer, but in practice. Bless others the way God blessed you. Your healed heart now has a voice—use it to honor Him. Gratitude strengthens what grace has started.

Thankfulness deepens transformation. When you appreciate God's mercy, your mindset shifts from one of regret to one of rejoicing. **Psalm 103:2** says, *"Bless the Lord... who forgives all your sins."* That means your past is gone, and praise must arise. Gratitude makes your spirit lighter, your steps bolder, and your love brighter. The more thankful you become, the stronger your faith grows. Don't just remember your mistake—remember your miracle. God didn't have to forgive—but He chose to. Celebrate that gift daily. Live with grateful boldness and peaceful praise.

Gratitude is also your testimony. When others see your joy, they'll ask what changed—and that's your moment to share. Your freedom points to His faithfulness. Your peace proves His promise. Every thank-you echoes eternity's anthem of grace. Say it. Show it. Spread it. Let every breath speak gratitude. Appreciate every ounce of mercy you've received. Then let that gratitude fuel your generosity, your gentleness, and your gospel. Forgiven people shine differently. Be the light that says, "God's mercy rescued me—and I'll never stop thanking Him."

6. Apply God's Word

God's Word is your weapon, your wisdom, and your wellspring. Don't just read it—release it. **Psalm 119:105** says, *"Your word is a lamp to my feet..."* meaning it lights every step in dark places. Scripture brings truth to confusion, power to weakness, and peace to pressure. To rise again, you need more than emotion—you need revelation. Let the Word become your guide. Open it daily. Speak it boldly. Stand on it firmly. The Bible doesn't just inspire—it instructs. And instruction leads to transformation.

Application brings activation. **James 1:22** challenges us—*"Do not merely listen... do what it says."* This is where victory happens—not just in hearing, but in doing. Let God's truth shape your decisions, your reactions, and your future. Take verses like seeds and plant them in your heart. Let faith grow through obedience. When you apply His Word, Heaven backs your steps. God honors what reflects His truth. Walk it out even when it's hard—because that's where strength is built. Action births alignment with God's will.

Your healing is rooted in truth. When the Word fills your heart, fear loses its grip. Temptation weakens, and wisdom awakens. Speak life—speak scripture—speak victory. Say, "I am more than a conqueror" (**Romans 8:37**). Say, "I can do all things..." (**Philippians 4:13**). Say what God says until you feel it, live it, and believe it. Let the Bible be your battle plan. Apply it in your mind, mouth, and mission. When you build your life on God's Word, even the strongest winds won't shake you.

7. Affirm and Anchor Your Faith

Affirmation is how you fight back against fear. Say who God says you are—loved, redeemed, strong, and restored. **Psalm 107:2** tells us, *"Let the redeemed of the Lord say so."* That's not just advice—it's a command. Speak life over yourself. Cancel the lies with truth. You are not broken—you are being rebuilt by grace. Affirm your identity until it becomes confidence. Say, "I am forgiven. I am chosen. I am healed." These words are seeds—plant them deep and repeat them often.

Words shape your walk. When you affirm God's truth, your spirit strengthens. Your healing requires a new language of faith. You're no longer defined by the fall—you're defined by your Father. Anchor your heart in what He says. **Hebrews 6:19** declares, *"We have this hope as an anchor..."* Faith keeps you grounded when feelings fluctuate. Say it even when you don't feel it. Say it until your spirit believes it. Speak truth until confidence rises. Your mouth can lead your heart to healing.

Affirming truth builds unshakable faith. You're not walking alone—you're anchored in God's promises. Let scripture be your foundation and your fortress. The storms may come, but anchored faith stands firm. Declare your hope. Declare your healing. Declare your identity. Say, "God is my refuge and strength" (**Psalm 46:1**). Say, "The Lord is my shepherd" (**Psalm 23:1**). Say it until your atmosphere changes. Anchor deep—and you'll rise higher. Because when faith is affirmed and anchored, your future becomes unstoppable.

8. Aspire to Grow and Glorify God

Aspire to rise—not just from the fall, but into a new purpose. You weren't created to be stuck—you were designed to soar. **Philippians 3:14** says, *"I press on toward the goal..."* That goal is not just success—it's surrender that leads to significance. Aspire to grow in grace, love, and wisdom. Your fall doesn't define your finish—it refines your faith. God uses brokenness to build boldness.

SYAVIHA MULENGYA

Aspire to live fully. Aspire to shine brightly. Aspire to glorify God in every step you take.

Growth is intentional. You must choose it, chase it, and cherish it. Don't settle for comfort—step into calling. God prunes so you can produce. **John 15:2** says He cuts what's holding you back to help you grow. Aspire to be teachable, faithful, and fruitful. Ask God to stretch your spirit. Your pain has prepared you for progress. Don't just return to what was—reach for what could be. Healing isn't about restoring the past—it's about building a future. So grow—upward, inward, and onward.

To glorify God is to live boldly for His name. **Colossians 3:23** says, *"Work at it with all your heart…"* That means every decision, every dream, and every detail can reflect Heaven. Aspire to be excellent—not to impress, but to impact. Aspire to live with joy, speak with grace, and serve with passion. God's glory shines through your growth. Let your life be worship. Aspire to influence with integrity and inspire with humility. You fell—but now you rise to glorify the One who never let go.

Sometimes we fall, but God is always ready to lift us up. First, we must **Recognize** our mistakes, like the prodigal son who *"came to himself"* (**Luke 15:17**) and saw his need to return home. Then we **Reflect**—thinking about what went wrong and what God wants us to learn. As we **Repent**, we turn back to God, just as He invites us: *"Return to me, and I will return to you"* (**Malachi 3:7**). When we **Release** pain, guilt, and fear to the Lord, we find peace. "Cast all your cares on Him, for He cares for you" (**1 Peter 5:7**).

After that, it's time to **Rebuild** with God's help. He promises, *"I will restore to you the years the locust has eaten"* (**Joel 2:25**). Even if life feels broken, God can renew your strength. You will **Rise** again! "Though he fall, he shall not be utterly cast down: for the Lord

SYAVIHA MULENGYA

upholdeth him with his hand" (**Psalm 37:24**). As you **Refocus**, set your heart on the Lord's purpose for your life. Let His Word guide your steps: *"Your word is a lamp to my feet and a light to my path"* (**Psalm 119:105**). With God, every fall becomes a setup for a greater comeback.

6

COME HOME, THE FATHER IS WAITING

*****

Come Back Home: The Father Is Waiting

No matter how far you've wandered, you are not beyond the reach of God's love. The story of the prodigal son (**Luke 15**) is not just a parable—it's a portrait of the Father's heart. It's about home, hope, and healing. When we run away, God doesn't reject us; He watches, waits, and welcomes. His love doesn't lecture—it embraces. His grace doesn't grow tired—it runs toward the broken. You may have wasted years, made mistakes, or doubted your worth. But the Father hasn't given up on you. He still calls you "son," still prepares a feast, still opens His arms. This is the sound of heaven: **"Come back home."** There's no punishment waiting—only restoration. So arise, return, and be renewed.

1. Drift Can Be Dangerous

Drifting doesn't always feel dramatic—it starts subtly, slowly pulling us away from the truth. The prodigal son didn't leap into rebellion overnight. It began with distance—a desire for control, for freedom without accountability. That drift led to disappointment, loss, and desperation. Sin sells dreams but delivers destruction.

SYAVIHA MULENGYA

When you disconnect from the Father, life loses its center. You forget who you are and what truly matters. In the far country, the son lost his dignity—but not his identity. He was still a son. God doesn't erase you when you drift—He waits to restore you. So beware the drift. And when you wake up in the pigpen, remember: home is still an option.

The danger of drifting is deception. It convinces you that the world has more to offer than God. It disguises bondage as freedom and emptiness as excitement. But separation from God never satisfies—it starves the soul. The further you go, the louder the pain becomes. Yet even in your drifting, divine mercy follows. **Psalm 139:7** says, *"Where can I go from Your Spirit?"* The answer is: nowhere. God's presence travels where you wander. His love outlasts your rebellion. So don't delay—if you've drifted, turn around. The Father hasn't moved, but He's waiting for your return. Today is your turning point.

2. Desire for Change Awakens Destiny

Change begins not with circumstances, but with desire. The prodigal didn't find healing in the pigpen—he found it when he said, *"I will arise."* That moment of desire was the doorway to destiny. You must want something different to step into something better. God won't force you—but He will wait for you. The first seed of transformation is a desire to be whole again. This longing is the whisper of grace awakening inside you. It's your spirit crying, "There's more than this." That cry is holy. It's the signal that Heaven is near and hope is rising.

Desire must become decision. Many feel regret, but few take action. The prodigal didn't stay stuck in sorrow—he chose to go back. Real change requires a response. You must move toward mercy. That step is faith in motion. God honors movement even if

SYAVIHA MULENGYA

your motives aren't perfect. **James 4:8** says, *"Draw near to God and He will draw near to you."* That's your promise. Let your desire drive your decision—and your decision define your direction. Don't wait until you feel worthy—come as you are, because the desire for change is a divine sign that destiny is still alive.

3. Decision to Return Restores Dignity

The moment the son headed home, restoration began. It wasn't the robe or the ring—it was the decision that changed everything. When you decide to return, Heaven responds immediately. You don't have to earn your way back—you only need to walk toward grace. That decision brings dignity. Shame loses its grip, and honor begins to rise. You may feel broken, but your decision makes you bold. The Father doesn't hold your failure against you—He heals it with love. Decide today: I'm coming home.

Returning restores what rebellion tried to steal. You are not a slave—you're still a son. That's what grace declares. When you decide to go back, the Father runs toward you. He doesn't just welcome you—He repositions you. **Isaiah 61:7** promises, *"Instead of shame, you will receive a double portion."* That's your inheritance. No matter the pit, your return unlocks the palace. Don't settle for guilt—step into glory. The power is not in the perfection of your journey, but in the decision to return to the One who never stopped loving you.

4. Demonstration of Grace Delivers Healing

The Father didn't wait behind a door; He ran down the road. That image shatters every lie about God being distant. His grace moves fast. It runs toward repentance, embracing the broken and celebrating the return. Healing doesn't come from distance; it flows from divine embrace. You don't have to explain, impress, or earn it.

SYAVIHA MULENGYA

The hug of Heaven is your healing. One touch of grace can undo years of guilt. Let God run to you.

Grace restores what the world tried to ruin. The son came home rehearsing shame—but the Father came out releasing restoration. That robe covered his filth. That ring restored his authority. That feast celebrated his value. Healing happens when grace is demonstrated, not just discussed. **Titus 2:11** says, *"The grace of God has appeared..."*—and it's for **you**. Don't dodge grace—let it deliver you. You may be wounded—but you're still wanted. Come back to grace and let healing begin.

5. Delight in Restoration Reflects Heaven

Heaven rejoices when the lost are found. The Father didn't respond with rebuke—He threw a party. That's how restoration looks in the kingdom: joyful, extravagant, public. Celebration is not foolish—it's biblical. God doesn't just forgive—He delights in doing it. **Luke 15:7** says, *"There is joy in Heaven over one sinner who repents."* When you come home, Heaven sings. That's your anthem: restoration deserves rejoicing.

Don't downplay your deliverance—delight in it. This joy is holy. It's the celebration of resurrection. You were dead in sin—but now you're alive in Christ. That deserves praise, not shame. The robe, ring, and feast were symbols—but your worship is your witness. Let others see your joy. Share your story. Sing your thanks. Heaven rejoiced over you—now you rejoice in Him. Restoration is not just private—it's praise-worthy. Let the celebration continue.

6. Danger of Bitterness Disrupts Blessing

The older brother missed the moment because he held onto resentment. Don't let bitterness blind you to grace. When others receive mercy, be glad—not jealous. Grace is not a competition—

SYAVIHA MULENGYA

it's a celebration. If you're busy counting faults, you'll miss the feast. Learn from this: bitterness disrupts blessings. It builds walls where God wants open doors.

Mercy received must become mercy given. The Father reminded the older son, *"All I have is yours."* That means there was never a need to feel threatened. Bitterness is rooted in insecurity. Love is rooted in identity. **Romans 12:15** says, *"Rejoice with those who rejoice..."* That includes the fallen who found freedom. Celebrate someone else's comeback—and yours will be even sweeter. Jealousy divides; joy multiplies. Guard your heart from comparison and open it to compassion.

7. Destiny Is Greater Than the Detour

The son didn't come home to just sit and regret—he came home to be restored. His destiny wasn't canceled by his detour. God's plan still stood. That's the beauty of redemption: grace not only erases the past—it empowers the future. You have a purpose after the pigpen. **Romans 11:29** says, *"God's gifts and calling are irrevocable."* Your mistake didn't remove your mission. You're still chosen.

Your detour becomes your ministry. What once hurt you now helps others. You know how to return—now teach others how to do the same. God will use your failure as fuel for someone else's faith. You are not just restored—you're repositioned. Your destiny was delayed, not denied. So rise, reclaim, and run your race. The Father is still calling—and your future is still unfolding.

Many people carry heavy struggles in silence, feeling ashamed or afraid to speak. But God wants us to come to Him honestly, just as we are. In **Matthew 11:28**, Jesus says, *"Come to Me, all you who are weary and burdened, and I will give you rest."* That means we don't need to hide our pain—we are invited to bring it. Your weakness doesn't push God away—it draws His grace closer. You are not alone, and you don't have to pretend. This chapter is a safe place where truth is honored and healing begins. No judgment, no rejection—only love. Don't be shy. There's peace waiting for those who choose to be real.

Struggles don't make you less—they make you human. Even great people in the Bible had moments of deep pain. David wept. Job questioned. Elijah felt hopeless. And yet, God listened, loved, and lifted them all. **Psalm 34:18** says, *"The Lord is close to the brokenhearted and saves those who are crushed in spirit."* Your struggles are not a barrier—they're a bridge to deeper grace. When you share, others find the courage to speak too. Healing flows when truth is spoken in love. Don't fear what people think—God thinks highly of you. Your story matters. Your tears have meaning. Speak boldly and let healing begin.

In **Luke 15,** the father ran to the broken son—not with anger, but with open arms. That's how God responds to us. He doesn't wait for perfect people—He waits for honest hearts. **Romans 10:13** says, *"Everyone who calls on the name of the Lord will be saved."* That includes you. All who come are welcome here. No matter your past, your pain, or your fear—you belong. You are not too far, too broken, or too late. So speak freely. Open your heart. There is room at the table. And the Father is waiting for you.

7

STOP BELIEVING LIES

*****

Many people believe the myth that their struggles mean God has left them, but that is not true. The Bible shows us again and again that God walks with us through trouble, not away from it. Joseph was betrayed, thrown into a pit, sold as a slave, and locked in prison—but God never abandoned him. Each painful moment shaped him for leadership and prepared him to save many lives. Paul suffered beatings, rejection, and hunger—but he still wrote, *"When I am weak, then I am strong"* (**2 Corinthians 12:10**). God's presence doesn't disappear in hard times—it becomes more powerful. Struggles don't prove weakness; they reveal strength. What you're facing now is not punishment— it is preparation.

Your struggle is not your shame—it's your shaping season. Don't accept the lie that you're forgotten or cursed. You are God's masterpiece in progress. The fire you face will not destroy you—it will refine your heart, your character, and your calling. The Bible says, *"After you have suffered a little while, He will restore, confirm, strengthen, and establish you"* (**1 Peter 5:10**). That is God's promise to you. You may feel stretched, broken, or worn—but God is

SYAVIHA MULENGYA

building something beautiful. You're not losing; you're learning. Every tear waters your testimony. Every scar will shine with proof that grace carried you through.

Sometimes God allows struggle so you can learn to lean on Him. He doesn't always remove the storm—but He teaches you how to stand in it. Just like the disciples in the boat, Jesus doesn't panic when the winds rise. He speaks peace and builds faith. Struggles teach trust. They teach prayer. They teach patience. And they grow spiritual muscles that comfort others later. **2 Corinthians 1:4** says that God comforts us so we can comfort those in trouble. Your pain now becomes your ministry later. So instead of asking, "Why me?" begin asking, "What is God building in me through this?"

The truth is: your story is not ending in struggle—it's rising in strength. Don't hide your hurt. Don't pretend to be perfect. Speak your story, stand in faith, and shine through grace. God did not abandon you. He is with you, for you, and working through you. **Isaiah 43:2** says, *"When you walk through the fire, you will not be burned…"* That means even when it's hard, He holds you close. Your testimony is forming. Your healing is happening. And your future is still unfolding. You are not broken—you are becoming. So take heart, take hope, and take one step closer to the God who never lets go.

1. See

The truth opens your spiritual eyes to recognize God's love, purpose, and direction. Without it, we walk in confusion. David prayed, *"Open my eyes that I may see wonderful things in Your law"* (**Psalm 119:18**). When you embrace the truth, lies lose their power, and light enters your heart. You begin to see your value, your calling, and your identity in Christ.

Lies try to blind you to your worth and keep you trapped in guilt, shame, and fear. But the truth breaks the fog and shines God's promises over your life. You are not forgotten—you are forgiven. You are not worthless—you are wonderfully made. You're not stuck—you're being shaped. What you see begins to change when you look through the lens of Scripture.

Seeing the truth doesn't just change your mind—it transforms your life. You no longer settle for less because you understand you were made for more. When you see clearly, you choose wisely. You don't chase approval—you walk with purpose. You don't react to lies—you respond with faith. God wants to open your eyes today so you can walk boldly toward the vision He placed in you.

2. Stand Up

Once your eyes are opened, it's time to rise. Truth is like a rock beneath your feet—it stabilizes you. Paul tells us in **Ephesians 6:13**, *"After you have done everything, to stand."* You don't have to bow to fear, confusion, or false accusations. You're called to stand— confidently, courageously, and consistently.

Lies push you down and make you question if you belong, but truth lifts your head. When you know God is with you, you don't collapse—you stand. You rise in prayer, in purpose, and in praise. You declare, "I'm not who I used to be—I'm redeemed." You may feel weak, but God gives grace to stand. You don't need strength from the world—you need truth from the Word.

Standing is not just resisting—it's revealing your faith. When you stand for truth, you become a testimony of God's faithfulness. You inspire others to rise. You show that hope is stronger than hurt. And you remind the enemy that you're not alone—heaven is backing your posture. So rise in the truth, and let your stand speak louder than any lie.

3. Silence the lies

The enemy is loud with lies, but God's Word is louder. Lies say you're not good enough, smart enough, spiritual enough—but truth says you're chosen, loved, and empowered. Jesus silenced the devil by saying, *"It is written…"* (**Matthew 4:4**). That's your weapon too—declare truth with confidence.

You don't argue with lies—you replace them. Every day, speak God's Word over your mind. Say, "I am strong. I am forgiven. I am equipped." Lies crumble when the truth is spoken boldly. Use Scripture as your sword. Lies sound convincing until God's promises cancel them out. Speak truth until the noise fades.

Silencing lies is a spiritual discipline. It's choosing to feed your faith and starve your fear. Lies will always knock—don't answer. Let God's truth dwell richly in you (**Colossians 3:16**). Your voice matters—so use it to declare victory. Truth not only breaks chains—it quiets the storms. Peace comes when truth reigns.

4. Step out

Truth doesn't just keep you steady—it propels you forward. **Psalm 119:105** says, *"Your Word is a lamp to my feet and a light to my path."* That means truth guides your steps. You don't need full clarity—just faith for the next step. Peter walked on water because he stepped into a word, not just a wave.

Lies keep you stuck, afraid to move. But truth says, "Go!" Step out of comfort, comparison, and control. Step into purpose, obedience, and destiny. Your step is an act of faith that activates heaven. Don't wait for perfect conditions—walk in perfect trust. Truth won't fail you. And God won't leave you halfway.

Every time you step with truth, you grow stronger. You build confidence, increase impact, and grow closer to the call on your life. Others may hesitate, but you move. The Bible says we walk by faith, not by sight (**2 Corinthians 5:7**). So take your step—it's time to walk into what God designed just for you.

5. Strengthen you

Truth is not just knowledge—it's nourishment. It strengthens your soul when life drains you. **Philippians 4:13** reminds us, *"I can do all things through Christ who strengthens me."* That strength doesn't come from hype—it comes from hope rooted in truth. Lies drain, but truth fuels.

When life feels heavy, the Word lifts. God's truth reminds you of His promises and restores your peace. You don't need perfect circumstances to feel strong—you need perfect truth. Even when you're tired, the truth revives. **Isaiah 40:31** says, *"They that wait upon the Lord shall renew their strength…"* So wait, read, pray, and be strengthened.

You don't have to pretend to be strong—just stay connected to the source. The more you lean on God's truth, the stronger you become. It's like planting your roots deep into God's faithfulness. You won't be shaken. Struggles may come—but strength will rise. Keep feeding on truth. It's your daily power.

6. Solve

Truth is not just spiritual—it's practical. It solves what stress complicates. Jesus said, *"You shall know the truth, and the truth shall set you free"* (**John 8:32**). Freedom solves pain. Faith solves panic. Truth shows a way out. It's not just about knowing—it's about applying.

God's Word answers life's questions. Confusion fades when truth enters. Lies multiply problems—but truth simplifies them. The Bible is full of strategies, promises, and solutions. You don't need worldly wisdom—you need divine truth. Ask God for insight and He will direct your steps (**Proverbs 3:5-6**).

Solving doesn't mean everything's easy—but everything's possible. God gives wisdom to those who ask (**James 1:5**). Don't guess—get guidance. Don't panic—pray. Truth always has an answer. It may not come instantly, but it will come faithfully. God's truth solves things with clarity, not chaos.

7. Shine & succeed

When you walk in truth, you shine. **Matthew 5:14** declares, *"You are the light of the world..."* You're not hidden—you're chosen to shine. Lies dim you—but truth reveals your light. The more truth you carry, the more hope you release. And that leads to true success in God's eyes.

Success is not just wealth or fame—it's walking in purpose and pleasing God. Lies chase applause, but truth seeks impact. When you live the truth, you succeed in fulfilling your calling. **Joshua 1:8** says meditating on the Word leads to success. That's God's promise—not just achievement but alignment.

You were born to shine. Not for ego—but for impact. Your light helps others find their way. Shine with kindness, love, and faith. Shine through struggles and testimonies. Success is not only surviving—it's thriving with truth. And every time you shine, the darkness loses again.

Truth activates and strengthens. In seasons of silence and storms, truth is not passive—it's powerful. It stands tall when emotion shakes, and it speaks when everything else falls quiet. Truth helps you stay planted like a tree by streams of living water (**Psalm 1:3**). It purifies like fire, sanctifying your thoughts and refining your heart. *"Sanctify them by Your truth; Your Word is truth"* (**John 17:17**). It invites surrender, not as a sign of weakness but worship. You release control and receive peace. It reveals through seeing and searching the Word, lifting the veil from your identity. Transformation begins when you don't just hear truth—but hold it, live it, and speak it boldly.

Truth creates movement and meaning. You were never meant to stay stuck in survival. Truth shifts your perspective, helps you step into purpose, and soars above fear. *"You will know the truth, and the truth will set you free"* (**John 8:32**). Freedom moves you forward. Truth simplifies what lies complicate—it clears the clutter of confusion. It aligns your actions with godly intentions, shaping decisions with discernment. You begin to serve with humility because truth removes pride. You support with strength, because truth builds character. Problems are solved by peace, not panic. And even when life grows quiet, truth begins to hum—faithful, gentle, and louder than fear.

Truth leads to fruitfulness and fulfillment. God doesn't just want you functional—He wants you flourishing. Truth is the seed that seals your destiny before the world sees the fruit. It builds your foundation like a house on rock (**Matthew 7:24**). It stirs your spirit—not just to survive the season, but to shine through it. You were made to rise above rejection, reflect His glory, and release hope to the hurting. The struggle is not the final word—truth speaks louder. When truth flows through your lips, lies lose power, and healing

SYAVIHA MULENGYA

finds a voice. Your testimony begins with truth—and ends in triumph.

8

SHARE YOUR STRUGGLES

*****

Share Without Shame

Many people hesitate to share their story because they fear judgment, rejection, or ridicule. They've been wounded by those who should have protected them—exposed instead of embraced. But God is not like people. When you open your heart to Him, He doesn't shame you—He shields you. He doesn't gossip about your past—He gently guides you into healing.

God invites honesty, not perfection. He already knows your story and still calls you His child. *"There is now no condemnation for those who are in Christ Jesus"* (**Romans 8:1**). You don't have to hide your pain or pretend to be strong. You can cry, confess, and come clean—because in His presence, there is safety and grace.

Sharing with God is sacred. He listens with love and responds with restoration. He doesn't use your past against you—He uses it to shape your purpose. *"You intended to harm me, but God intended it for good"* (**Genesis 50:20**). What others may use to hurt you, God will use to help you grow.

So speak freely. Share boldly. Let your story become a testimony. You are not alone, and you are not ashamed. You are accepted, loved, and welcome.

3. Stop Struggling Alone

You've been carrying burdens no one sees. You smile in public but cry in private. You've been strong for others, yet inside, you feel weak and weary. God sees your silent struggle, and He wants to walk with you through it.

You don't have to fight alone. You don't have to pretend everything is fine. God is your refuge, your strength, and your support. *"God is our refuge and strength, an ever-present help in trouble"* (**Psalm 46:1**). He understands your pain even when you can't put it into words.

When you invite God into your struggle, you gain supernatural strength. He lifts what you can't carry. He comforts what you can't explain. He brings peace to your storm and light to your darkness. *"Cast all your anxiety on Him because He cares for you"* (**1 Peter 5:7**).

So stop hiding. Stop hurting in silence. Let God in. Let Him help. You are not forgotten. You are not forsaken. You are deeply loved— and you are welcome.

4. Speak to God Who Has Solution

You've been searching for answers in people, places, and possessions. But nothing satisfies. That's because the solution isn't found in things; it's found in God. He is the answer to your deepest questions and the healer of your deepest wounds.

God knows what you need before you ask. He understands your confusion, your longing, and your desire for peace. *"Before*

SYAVIHA MULENGYA

they call I will answer; while they are still speaking I will hear" (**Isaiah 65:24**). He doesn't offer temporary relief; He offers lasting restoration.

When you turn to God, you find clarity, comfort, and the courage to move forward. He gives you wisdom for your decisions, strength for your battles, and hope for your future. *"Trust in the Lord with all your heart and lean not on your own understanding"* (**Proverbs 3:5**). He is not distant; He is near. He is not silent; He is speaking.

So stop searching in the wrong places. Start seeking the right Person. God is the solution you've been looking for. And He's ready to walk with you. You are welcome

9

YOU DESERVE FREEDOM

*****

Because **Freedom Is God's Design for You.** From the beginning, God created you for fellowship, not bondage—for walking with Him, not wandering in chains. The Bible says in **Galatians 5:1**, *"It is for freedom that Christ has set us free."* That freedom isn't just from external oppression—it's freedom from guilt, sin, shame, fear, and lies. You were never meant to live trapped by what others said or what mistakes tried to define. God designed you for peace, purpose, and power. When you're bound, you can't fully succeed—but freedom gives you wings. Just like the Israelites were delivered from Egypt to worship freely, God wants you delivered to dwell freely in His presence.

Because Freedom Allows You to Fulfill Your Purpose. Bondage breaks focus, but freedom restores vision. When God sets you free, you begin to see who you really are: chosen, called, and capable. *"You are a royal priesthood, a holy nation, God's special possession..."* (**1 Peter 2:9**). That's not just poetry—it's your position. You can't reach your destiny while dragging chains. Freedom helps you serve, shine, and succeed in what God has placed inside you. God wants to see you rise, not just survive. And

SYAVIHA MULENGYA

every time He frees a soul, heaven rejoices because the testimony is ready to touch others.

Because Freedom Is the Mark of His Love and Power. God isn't glorified by your defeat; He's glorified by your deliverance. That's why Jesus declared in **John 8:36**, *"If the Son sets you free, you will be free indeed."* True freedom is not just behavior change—it's heart transformation. God wants you whole, healed, and holy—not hiding, hurting, or held back. He breaks chains not just to prove His strength, but to express His love. Your freedom declares His victory. It shows the world that grace wins. When you're free, you worship deeper, live bolder, and walk wiser. And that kind of freedom turns your life into a light for others.

"Come to Me, all…" (**Matthew 11:28**). That means every soul, every story, every struggle. God's love welcomes all, not with judgment, but with joy. He doesn't just want you near; He wants you free. Free to live, laugh, love, and walk in purpose. You were created to be happy, healthy, and hopeful. And that is why God offers true freedom—not temporary relief, but lasting breakthrough. Your freedom is the beginning of your fruitfulness. When you walk in liberty, you stand tall, shine bright, and serve well.

1. Peace

Freedom begins with peace. Not the kind the world gives—but deep, soul-settling peace. Jesus said, *"My peace I give you…"* (**John 14:27**). In freedom, anxiety fades and rest takes its place. Peace brings calm to storms and clarity to chaos. It's the gentle assurance that you are held by God. You no longer strive—you simply trust. Worry loses its grip, and worship rises. God's freedom covers your heart like a soft blanket on a cold night. You don't have to figure everything out—you just need to lean in.

SYAVIHA MULENGYA

Peace guards your heart and mind. **Philippians 4:7** says, *"The peace of God... will guard your hearts."* That means peace isn't passive—it's protective. It defends your joy from fear and your thoughts from confusion. You sleep better, breathe deeper, and live stronger. Peace is proof that God is present—even when life gets loud. It creates stillness that fuels strength. Peace clears the path for purpose.

When God sets you free, peace becomes your atmosphere. It changes how you respond, how you relate, and how you recover. You don't panic when problems come—you pray. You don't explode when pressured—you endure. Peace makes you unshakable. You may not control every situation, but with peace, you rise above it. Free people walk with grace, not grumbling.

Peace allows you to live without fear of the past or dread of the future. You stop replaying old pain and start singing new songs. **Psalm 29:11** says, *"The Lord blesses His people with peace."* That's your inheritance. Peace is not the absence of trouble—it's the presence of Jesus. And in that presence, freedom flows like a river. Let it carry you.

2. Purpose

Freedom gives you clarity—your life has meaning. You're not here by accident but by divine assignment. **Jeremiah 29:11** says, *"For I know the plans I have for you..."* That means God has a purpose—and your freedom helps you pursue it. You are not chasing approval; you're carrying destiny. In bondage, purpose feels distant. But freedom brings it close.

Purpose makes your life intentional. You wake up with direction, not distraction. You serve with joy, not just out of duty. You begin to see your gifts, your calling, and your role in God's story.

Freedom unlocks creativity and courage. You stop hiding, start helping, and heal as you go. Your life becomes a light in the darkness.

Knowing your purpose gives you boldness. You stop saying, "I'm not enough," and start declaring, "I am called." You walk into rooms with confidence because God is with you. You stop apologizing for your existence and start honoring your assignment. Purpose turns weakness into strength and wandering into worship.

Purpose also keeps you grounded when storms hit. You're not shaken because you're rooted. Romans 8:28 reminds us that *"all things work together..."* when you love God and walk in purpose. That includes setbacks, struggles, and seasons of silence. Your freedom leads you to impact, influence, and intimacy with the Father. Live with purpose—your story matters.

3. Power

Freedom activates divine power in your life. Acts 1:8 says, *"You will receive power when the Holy Spirit comes upon you."* That power gives you courage to speak, strength to stand, and wisdom to lead. You're no longer living by your own efforts—but by God's energy. Power doesn't mean loud—it means life-changing.

God's power helps you overcome temptation and speak truth boldly. It silences fear and drives out spiritual darkness. When you know who you are and whose you are, you become unstoppable. You walk in spiritual authority—not pride, but presence. You don't back down—you rise up. Power helps you say "no" to bondage and "yes" to blessing.

Power fuels your purpose. It gives you endurance for the race and fire for the fight. You're not drained—you're driven. You pray with power. You sing with strength. You serve with joy. You don't just talk about freedom—you live it. Power isn't about control—it's about capacity. God enlarges your ability to love, lead, and last.

When God gives you power, He also gives you protection. **Isaiah 54:17** says, *"No weapon formed against you shall prosper."* That means you're covered. Power is not physical—it's spiritual. It fights battles you can't see and wins victories you didn't expect. So walk boldly—God's power is your portion.

4. Progress

Freedom doesn't mean perfection—it means movement. You're not stuck, you're stepping forward. **Proverbs 4:18** says, *"The path of the righteous is like the morning sun, shining ever brighter..."* You may not be where you want to be, but you're not where you used to be. That's progress. Celebrate it.

Progress means you learn, grow, and rise with each step. You make wiser choices and recover faster from setbacks. You don't let past mistakes hold you in place. You forgive, release, and rebuild. You let God rewrite the chapters shame tried to end. Progress isn't always easy—but it's always worth it.

God gives grace for the journey, not just the destination. You don't have to rush—you just have to trust. **Psalm 84:7** says, *"They go from strength to strength..."* That means progress comes in stages. Some days are quiet, some are loud, but all are holy. Each step forward brings wisdom and strength.

Freedom creates progress that leads to promotion. Like Joseph in Egypt, your setbacks may be long—but your comeback is strong. You keep going because God is guiding. You don't stay stuck—you step up. Progress honors the process, and the process reveals God's promise. So keep moving forward—your future is bright.

5. Productivity

Freedom clears your mind and frees your time. When you're no longer battling guilt or regret, your energy flows toward building and blessing. **Colossians 3:23** says, *"Whatever you do, work at it with all your heart..."* Freedom empowers you to focus, follow through, and flourish. No more delays—just divine drive.

Productivity is not about doing more—it's about doing what matters. You start writing, creating, and connecting with purpose. You begin organizing your days around obedience and impact. God doesn't rush you—He refines you. In freedom, your priorities shift and your pace improves. You work with wisdom, not weariness.

When you're productive, you multiply blessings. Like the servants in the parable of the talents, freedom enables fruitfulness (**Matthew 25:14-30**). You grow your gifts, steward your resources, and serve others with excellence. No longer stuck—you're stirred. You stop complaining and start creating. Freedom awakens holy hustle.

God wants you to be productive so that you can bless others, build the Kingdom, and leave a lasting legacy. **Proverbs 31:17** praises the woman who "sets about her work vigorously." That's you—empowered, engaged, effective. In freedom, your work becomes worship. And your impact echoes for generations.

6. Potential

Freedom unleashes your hidden treasures. You stop settling and start soaring. **Ephesians 2:10** says, *"We are His workmanship..."* That means you're a masterpiece, packed with purpose. In bondage, potential stays buried—but in freedom, it blooms. You grow into greatness.

SYAVIHA MULENGYA

You have gifts, talents, and ideas waiting to be explored. Freedom gives you space to experiment and express. You write songs, speak truth, teach boldly, and lead wisely. You stop mimicking others and start mastering your own voice. Your uniqueness becomes your strength.

Potential stretches you. You begin to try things you once feared. You say "yes" to growth and "no" to limits. You explore, expand, and elevate. You stop shrinking and start shining. God's Spirit becomes your fuel, and nothing is impossible. With Christ, you can climb higher.

Your potential isn't just personal—it's prophetic. **Romans 8:19** says creation waits for the sons of God to be revealed. That's you. Your freedom makes room for miracles. You build, bless, and bring transformation to people and places. So rise up—your potential is powerful.

7. Protection

Freedom covers you. It shields you from spiritual attacks, emotional manipulation, and environmental oppression. **Psalm 91:4** says, *"He will cover you with His feathers…"* That means God's protection is both strong and soft. You don't have to fear the fire—you walk through it untouched.

Protection means God is your defender. You don't fight alone. You trust, not tremble. You rest while He resists the enemy. **Isaiah 41:10** says, *"Do not fear, for I am with you…"* That promise is your fortress. Freedom places you under divine insurance. You're surrounded.

Freedom also protects your mind. You stop believing lies and start declaring truth. You put on the helmet of salvation and the shield of faith (**Ephesians 6:17**). God guards your peace and preserves your purpose. You stop reacting to everything—and start relying on Him. Protected people are peaceful people.

Protection doesn't mean trouble disappears; it means it doesn't destroy you. Like Daniel in the lion's den or the Hebrew boys in the fire, freedom ensures survival. You walk through storms but stay secure. You stand in adversity but remain anchored. God's protection is your portion.

8. Profit

Freedom leads to fruitfulness. You don't just survive—you succeed. **Deuteronomy 8:18** says, *"It is He who gives you power to get wealth…"* That wealth is not just money—it's momentum, meaning, and multiplication. You prosper in soul, body, and ministry.

Profit isn't greed—it's growth. You steward resources well, bless others freely, and build wisely. You stop wasting and start investing. You recognize open doors and walk through them boldly. God gives you ideas and increases your influence. Your freedom becomes your fuel for favor.

Profit also means impact. You help others rise. Your gifts create jobs, your songs inspire souls, and your books change lives. You're not chasing success—you're carrying blessing. Like Joseph, what once looked like a setback becomes a setup. Your profit is prophetic.

God wants you to prosper because it displays His goodness. **Psalm 1:3** says, *"In all that he does, he prospers."* That's the testimony of the free. You reap where you sow, and you sow with joy. Your profit becomes praise. Keep planting—harvest is near.

9. Praise

Freedom makes you worship with joy. **Psalm 98:4** says, *"Shout for joy to the Lord…"* When you're no longer burdened by shame or sin, your praise flows naturally. You don't hold back—you lift up. Freedom fuels celebration. You sing because you're seen. You dance because you're delivered.

Praise breaks chains. When Paul and Silas praised in prison, the walls shook and doors opened (**Acts 16:25-26**). That's freedom at work. Your worship isn't just emotional—it's explosive. When you praise, breakthroughs happen. Praise isn't a performance—it's a weapon.

Free people praise without fear. They don't worry about approval—they adore the Almighty. They don't compare—they connect. Praise becomes their heartbeat. You praise in the pain and in the progress. You praise not because everything's perfect, but because God is present.

Praise also becomes your platform. You inspire others to rejoice, reflect, and rise. Your story becomes a song. Your struggle becomes a shout. You point people to God—not with sermons, but with sincerity. So lift your voice—praise is your portion.

10. Positive Perception

Freedom transforms how you see—yourself, others, and life. You stop seeing through pain and start seeing through purpose. **2 Corinthians 5:17** reminds us, *"If anyone is in Christ… the old has gone, the new is here!"* That means new lenses. You see with hope, not hurt.

Positive perception means you believe the best—not blindly, but boldly. You recognize growth even in brokenness. You speak life even in lack. You see potential even in problems. Freedom rewires your mind. You stop replaying defeat and start declaring victory.

When your perception changes, so does your posture. You stand taller, smile wider, and walk stronger. You respond with grace, not grudges. You celebrate others instead of competing. You stop assuming the worst and start anticipating wonders. Free minds think higher.

God wants you to see as He sees—pure, powerful, and purposeful. **Proverbs 3:5-6** tells us to trust and not lean on our own understanding. Freedom helps you do that. You perceive with faith, not fear. You live with clarity and conviction. Your vision becomes your victory.

All who come are welcome—no conditions, no credentials, just a heart willing to receive. Jesus declared in **John 6:37**, *"Whoever comes to Me I will never drive away."* That includes the weary, wounded, and wandering. God is not exclusive—He is expansive. He receives, restores, and renews every soul. You are recognized as His child, revealed in purpose, and rewarded with peace. This freedom is not forced—it's freely given. It's not flimsy—it's firm and eternal. All are invited to embrace true freedom—the kind that replaces fear with faith.

What Freedom Gives You

This divine freedom opens the door to peace that calms storms, purpose that directs destiny, and power that breaks chains. It provides protection in every battle, provision in every valley, and profit that multiplies your impact. **Galatians 5:1** reminds us, *"It is for freedom that Christ has set us free..."* You're no longer held—you're healed. In this freedom, your life is fruitful, fearless, and favored. You shine, stand out, and serve well. Your freedom makes you firm in storms, fair in choices, and faithful in calling. God's freedom isn't shallow—it's supernatural.

SYAVIHA MULENGYA

Freedom from God isn't a concept—it's a covenant. It lifts burdens, loosens bonds, and launches blessings. It's the freedom that gives you confidence to walk boldly, speak truthfully, and love deeply. **Romans 8:15** says, *"You did not receive the spirit of bondage again to fear, but... the Spirit of adoption."* That means you are chosen, cherished, and changed. You live with vision, not a victim mentality. You embrace identity over insecurity. This is the best freedom—the kind that outlasts circumstances and overcomes condemnation. You don't just have freedom—you live it fearlessly.

10

LET GOD LEAD YOU

*****

Start with God: A Strong and Sure Beginning

Starting with God means putting Him first in your life. He is the Creator of everything—He knows all things, owns all things, and can do all things. When you begin with God, you are choosing the best foundation for your life. You are saying, "God, I need You to lead me, help me, and walk with me." The Bible says, *"In the beginning, God…"* (**Genesis 1:1**). That means everything starts with Him—including you.

When you start with God, you receive peace, power, protection, and provision. His peace calms your heart. His power gives you strength. His protection keeps you safe. His provision meets your needs. **Psalm 23:1** says, *"The Lord is my shepherd; I shall not want."* That means when God leads you, you will not lack anything. He knows what is best for you and will guide you step by step.

Starting with God also gives you direction. Life can be confusing, but God shows you the right way. **Proverbs 3:5–6** says, *"Trust in the Lord with all your heart… and He will direct your paths."* When you trust Him, He helps you make good choices. He opens doors, closes wrong ones, and leads you to your purpose.

Why is it important to start with God? Because He is the only one who never fails. Money, people, and fame may come and go, but God remains faithful. He gives you hope that lasts. **Jeremiah 29:11** says, *"For I know the plans I have for you… plans to give you hope and a future."* When you start with God, you start with a future full of promise.

How do you start with God? You open your heart to Him. You pray and talk to Him. You read the Bible to know His voice. You trust Him and follow His ways. You don't need to be perfect—just willing. **James 4:8** says, *"Draw near to God, and He will draw near to you."* That means if you take one step toward Him, He will come close to you.

Starting with God is the best decision you can make. It brings peace to your heart, strength to your walk, and joy to your journey. Whether you are starting a new day, a new dream, or a new direction—start with God. He will never leave you, and He will never let you down

1. Invite God

To invite God means to welcome Him into every part of your life. It's saying, "Lord, I need You. Come into my heart, my home, my plans, and my decisions." This is the first and most important step in building a strong relationship with Him. **Revelation 3:20** says, *"Behold, I stand at the door and knock. If anyone hears My voice and opens the door, I will come in…"* God is waiting for your invitation. He doesn't force His way in—He responds to your open heart.

ALL WHO COME ARE WELCOME | 76

When you invite God, you are choosing to let Him lead. You are saying, "Not my will, but Yours be done." This brings peace and confidence, because you know He is in control. **Psalm 127:1** reminds us, *"Unless the Lord builds the house, the builders labor in vain."* Starting with God means building with purpose, not pressure. It means trusting His timing, His wisdom, and His way.

Inviting God also means trusting Him with your future. You may not know what tomorrow holds, but you know who holds tomorrow. When you begin with God, you begin with hope. He will walk with you, work through you, and lead you to success. **Proverbs 16:3** says, *"Commit to the Lord whatever you do, and He will establish your plans."* When God is invited, success is guaranteed.

2. Involve God

To involve God means to include Him in everything you do—not just in emergencies, but in everyday life. **Proverbs 3:6** says, *"In all your ways acknowledge Him, and He will direct your paths."* God wants to be part of your plans, your work, your relationships, and your dreams. He is not just a Sunday God—He is a daily guide.

Involving God means seeking His wisdom before making decisions. Whether it's about your family, finances, or future, ask Him to lead you. He sees what you cannot see and knows what you do not know. **Isaiah 48:17** says, *"I am the Lord your God, who teaches you what is best for you, who directs you in the way you should go."* When you involve Him, you avoid many mistakes and walk in divine favor.

It also means serving with Him. Use your gifts to bless others and build His Kingdom. **Colossians 3:17** says, *"Whatever you do… do it all in the name of the Lord Jesus."* When God is involved, your work becomes worship, and your efforts bring eternal impact. You are not working alone—God is working through you.

3. Inquiry Before God

Inquiry means asking questions, seeking answers, and searching for truth. God invites us to ask. **James 1:5** says, *"If any of you lacks wisdom, let him ask of God, who gives generously…"* He is ready to give you insight, direction, and understanding. Asking God shows that you trust His knowledge more than your own.

When you inquire of God, you show humility. You admit, "I don't know everything, but I know the One who does." This opens the door to divine guidance. David often asked God before making decisions, and God gave him victory. In **1 Samuel 23:2**, David asked, *"Shall I go and attack these Philistines?"* and God answered him clearly. Inquiry leads to clarity.

Inquiry also means studying His Word. The Bible is full of answers. **Psalm 119:105** says, *"Your word is a lamp to my feet and a light to my path."* When you search the Scriptures, you find wisdom for life, strength for trials, and clarity for your calling. God speaks through His Word, and those who inquire grow in truth.

4. Intercede

Intercession means praying for others. It's standing in the gap for your family, friends, community, and nation. **1 Timothy 2:1** says, *"I urge… that prayers, intercession… be made for all people."* God listens when you pray with love and faith. Your prayers can change lives and shift situations.

When you intercede, you become a channel of blessing. Your prayers can bring healing, protection, and breakthrough to others. Abraham interceded for Sodom, Moses for Israel, and Jesus for all of us. You are called to do the same. **Ezekiel 22:30** says, *"I looked for someone... who would stand before Me in the gap..."* God is still looking for intercessors today.

Intercession also builds compassion. As you pray for others, your heart becomes more like God's. **Galatians 6:2** says, *"Carry each other's burdens, and in this way you will fulfill the law of Christ."* When you intercede, you reflect God's love and help bring His will to earth. You become a spiritual warrior and a vessel of grace.

5. Incline Toward God

To incline means to lean in and listen. **Isaiah 55:3** says, *"Incline your ear, and come to Me; hear, that your soul may live."* God speaks, but we must be willing to hear. When you incline your heart, you become sensitive to His voice. Listening is the key to learning and growing.

Inclining also means being teachable. You allow God to correct, guide, and shape you. **Psalm 25:4-5** says, *"Show me Your ways, Lord... teach me Your paths."* A humble heart is a listening heart, and a listening heart is a growing heart. God speaks through His Word, His Spirit, and His servants.

Finally, inclining means staying close. You don't just hear once—you keep listening. You stay in His Word, stay in prayer, and stay in step with His Spirit. **John 10:27** says, *"My sheep hear My voice, and I know them, and they follow Me."* When you incline toward God, you walk in wisdom, avoid confusion, and live in victory.

SYAVIHA MULENGYA

11

I AM OK, BUT I AM NOT OK — REMOVE THE MASK

*****

Many people live behind masks, smiling on the outside while suffering on the inside. They say, "I'm fine," while silently crying for help. They lead ministries, raise families, and carry responsibilities, yet inside they feel overwhelmed, anxious, and alone. The mask becomes their shield, their survival tool, their silent cry for dignity. But God sees behind the mask. He knows the real you—and still loves you deeply.

You don't have to pretend with God. You don't have to perform or impress Him. He's not looking for perfection—He's looking for honesty. *"You desire truth in the inward parts"* (**Psalm 51:6**). When you remove the mask, you make room for healing. When you stop hiding, you start healing. Vulnerability is not weakness—it's the doorway to restoration.

God welcomes your truth. He embraces your vulnerability. He doesn't reject the broken parts of you—He restores them. *"He heals the brokenhearted and binds up their wounds"* (**Psalm 147:3**). You are not too messy for His mercy. You are not too flawed for His favor. In fact, the very areas you try to hide are the ones He longs to heal.

So be real. Be open. Be free. Take off the mask and let God touch the places you've been hiding. In His presence, you are safe, seen, and secure. You are welcome just as you are. And when you are honest with God, you'll find the courage to be honest with others—and that honesty will lead to deeper connection, healing, and hope.

I Am Fine, But I Am Not OK

Sometimes we smile, serve, and speak with strength, yet inside we feel stretched, shaken, or silently suffering. We say "I'm OK" to keep moving, but deep down, we know something is missing. This is not weakness—it's a cry for deeper healing, hope, and help. Even David, a man after God's heart, said, *"Why are you cast down, O my soul?"* (**Psalm 42:5**). He was honest with God—and that honesty led to restoration.

Being "not OK" is not the end—it's an invitation to start again with God. He sees behind the mask, hears the silent prayers, and understands the pain we cannot explain. Jesus said, *"Come to Me, all who are weary and burdened, and I will give you rest."* (**Matthew 11:28**). When we come to Him as we are, He meets us with grace, not judgment—with healing, not shame.

So if you're saying, "I am OK, but I am not OK," know this: God is not distant. He is near to the brokenhearted (**Psalm 34:18**). You don't have to pretend with Him. You can invite Him into the hidden places. He will restore your soul, renew your strength, and remind you—you are not alone, and you are not forgotten.

Why People Wear Masks

1. Shame

Shame is a silent prison. It doesn't just whisper—it screams in the soul, "You're not enough." It convinces people to cover up, to pretend, to perform. Many walk into churches, homes, and workplaces with bright smiles but broken hearts. They fear that if others knew their past, their pain, or their private struggles, they'd be cast aside. So they wear the mask—not because they want to deceive, but because they're desperate to belong.

But shame is not from God. It's a tool of the enemy to keep us bound. God doesn't shame—He saves. *"Anyone who believes in Him will never be put to shame"* (**Romans 10:11**). That's a promise. When we come to God, He doesn't expose us to embarrass us—He reveals us to restore us. He doesn't see a failure—He sees a future. He doesn't see a mess—He sees a miracle in the making.

People hide behind shame because they've been hurt before. Maybe someone betrayed their trust, mocked their vulnerability, or used their story against them. So now, they stay silent. They isolate. They pretend. But healing begins when we stop hiding. Shame loses its grip when we step into the light of God's love.

Jesus didn't run from the ashamed—He ran toward them. He touched the leper, spoke to the adulterer, and welcomed the outcast. He didn't just forgive—He restored dignity. That same Jesus is reaching for you today. He knows your story, and He still says, "Come."

If you feel ashamed, remember: you are not alone. You are not beyond healing. You are not defined by your worst moment. God invites you to come as you are. He will not expose you—He will embrace you. You are welcome. You are worthy. You are wonderfully loved.

SYAVIHA MULENGYA

Let shame be silenced by grace. Let guilt be replaced by glory. Let your story be a testimony, not a tragedy. You are not what happened to you—you are who God says you are. And He says, "You are mine."

2. Sin

Sin separates. It creates a gap between us and God, between us and others, and even between us and ourselves. When someone falls, the instinct is to hide. To cover up. To pretend it didn't happen. They fear judgment, rejection, or being labeled. But hiding sin doesn't heal it—it multiplies the pain. The longer it stays in the dark, the stronger its grip becomes. God doesn't turn away from sinners—He runs toward them. *"While we were still sinners, Christ died for us"* (**Romans 5:8**). That means He didn't wait for us to clean up—He came to clean us up. His love is not based on our performance—it's based on His promise. His grace is greater than any mistake. His mercy is deeper than any mess.

People often think they must fix themselves before coming to God. But that's not the gospel. The gospel says, "Come now." God doesn't wait for perfection—He responds to repentance. Confession is not weakness—it's wisdom. It opens the door to freedom, healing, and peace. It's not about punishment—it's about restoration. Sin thrives in secrecy. But when we bring it into the light, it loses its power. God doesn't condemn—He cleanses. He doesn't shame—He sanctifies. He doesn't discard—He delivers. The blood of Jesus is not just enough—it's more than enough.

If you're hiding sin, don't stay in the dark. Bring it to God. He already knows—and He still loves you. You are not too far gone. You are not beyond redemption. You are welcome. You are forgiven. You are free. Let today be the day you stop running and start returning.

SYAVIHA MULENGYA

God is not angry—He's waiting. He's not distant—He's near. He's not disappointed—He's devoted. Come home.

3. Secrets

Secrets are heavy. They weigh down the heart, cloud the mind, and steal joy. People often hide their past, pain, or truth because they fear being misunderstood or judged. They smile on the outside but carry silent stories inside. Secrets can feel safer than honesty—but they also keep us stuck. They isolate us from intimacy and rob us of real connection.

God sees what others cannot. *"Nothing in all creation is hidden from God's sight"* (**Hebrews 4:13**). Yet He doesn't use that knowledge to shame us—He uses it to heal us. He knows every detail and still calls us His. He doesn't flinch at our truth—He embraces it. He doesn't recoil—He reaches.

Secrets often grow when we stay silent. In the dark, they feel heavier and louder. But when we bring them to God, they lose their power. He gives us safety instead of shame, and freedom instead of fear. You don't have to carry it alone. There's no need to pretend or hide. God already knows your story, and He still wants to help. Many people keep secrets because they've been hurt before. Maybe someone broke their trust. Maybe they were judged or told to stay quiet. But God is not like people. He is kind, gentle, and faithful. He doesn't spread your secrets—He protects your heart.

If you're holding something inside, let God hold you. He is strong enough to carry your truth and gentle enough to heal your pain. With Him, you are safe. You are welcome. You are seen. You are loved. What stays hidden cannot be healed. But when you bring it to God, He can restore it. Let your secret become the start of healing. Let your silence turn into peace. You are not your mistake or your past. You are God's child. And He still says, "You are mine."

6. Stigma

Stigma is a silent shadow. It follows people who've been labeled, misunderstood, or marginalized. It tells them they're "too different," "too broken," or "too far gone." Whether it's mental health, addiction, divorce, or poverty, society often stamps people with shame. And so, they hide. Not because they want to, but because they feel they have to.

God doesn't label—He liberates. He doesn't see categories—He sees children. *"There is no condemnation for those who are in Christ Jesus"* (**Romans 8:1**). That means your past doesn't define you—His promise does. Jesus broke every barrier, touched every outcast, and welcomed every soul. He didn't avoid stigma—He confronted it with love.

People hide behind stigma because they've been hurt by judgment. Maybe someone made a cruel comment. Maybe they were excluded from a group. Maybe they were treated as less. But God doesn't treat us based on public opinion—He treats us based on divine compassion.

Stigma can silence stories and make people feel unseen. It causes pain that others may not notice. But God sees what others miss. He hears the quiet cries and understands the hidden hurt. Every voice matters to Him, even the ones the world tries to silence. You are more than a diagnosis. You are not defined by past mistakes. Your worth is not tied to your reputation. You belong to God.

If shame has kept you in hiding, know this—God welcomes you with open arms. He doesn't turn away from your story; He draws near. You are not alone in your struggle. You are remembered,

SYAVIHA MULENGYA

accepted, and loved. Truth breaks the grip of stigma. Love replaces every label. Your life can shine and bring hope to others who feel forgotten. The world may speak lies, but God speaks truth. And His message is clear: "You are mine."

7. Skepticism

Skepticism is a shield. It's built from disappointment, betrayal, and broken trust. People become skeptical when promises are broken, when leaders fail, or when love hurts. They stop believing, stop hoping, and stop trusting. They wear the mask—not to deceive—but to protect their fragile faith.

God understands skepticism. Even Thomas doubted, and Jesus didn't rebuke him—He revealed Himself. *"Blessed are those who have not seen and yet have believed"* (**John 20:29**). God doesn't demand blind faith—He invites honest questions. He meets us in our doubt and leads us to deeper belief. People hide behind skepticism because they've been let down. Maybe they prayed and didn't see results. Maybe they trusted someone who betrayed them. Maybe they believed in something that failed. So now, they guard their heart. They smile, but they don't open up.

God is not like people. He is always faithful, always true, and always trustworthy. Unlike man, He never lies, never changes, and never lets us down. His character stays the same—strong, steady, and good. He invites us to come close, to ask, to seek, and to know Him. Those who do discover His kindness and strength. If doubt has kept you distant, let Him show you who He really is. Questions don't scare Him. Honest thoughts don't push Him away. He welcomes the curious and comforts the unsure. Healing begins when we stop hiding. Trust grows when we see His heart. Even with your questions, you are still welcome.

SYAVIHA MULENGYA

Let your questions lead you closer to God. Let your doubts turn into honest talks with Him. Open your heart and let faith grow inside. God is not far away—He is right here. And He gently says, "Come close."

8. Status

Status is a mask of performance. People hide behind titles, achievements, and appearances. They feel pressure to look successful, sound confident, and seem perfect. They fear that if they show weakness, they'll lose respect. So they keep up the image—even when they're falling apart inside.

But God doesn't care about status—He cares about surrender. *"Man looks at the outward appearance, but the Lord looks at the heart"* (**1 Samuel 16:7**). He's not impressed by titles—He's moved by truth. He doesn't reward performance—He responds to humility. People hide behind status because they've been taught that worth comes from work. That value comes from visibility. That success equals significance. But God flips the script. He says the last will be first, the humble will be lifted, and the broken will be blessed.

Status can be exhausting. It demands perfection, applause, and constant effort. But God offers rest. He says, "Come to Me, all who are weary, and I will give you rest" (**Matthew 11:28**). You don't have to prove yourself—you just have to present yourself.

If you're hiding behind status, let God strip away the pressure. You are not your job, your title, or your bank account. You are His beloved. You are welcome—not because of what you've done, but because of who He is.

Let status be replaced by surrender. Let performance be replaced by peace. Let your identity be rooted in grace, not grind. You are enough. You are accepted. You are welcome.

SYAVIHA MULENGYA

9. Solitude

Solitude can be sacred—but it can also be a shield. Some people isolate not because they enjoy being alone, but because they fear being exposed. They've been hurt, misunderstood, or rejected. So they retreat. They build walls instead of bridges. They say, "I'm OK," but inside, they're aching.

God sees the lonely. *"God sets the lonely in families"* **(Psalm 68:6)**. He doesn't ignore isolation—He invades it with love. Jesus often withdrew to pray, but He never abandoned people. He walked with the broken, sat with the rejected, and welcomed the weary.

People hide in solitude because they've been wounded by relationships. Maybe they were betrayed. Maybe they were judged. Maybe they were abandoned. So now, they protect their heart by keeping them hidden. But healing happens in connection. God created us for community. For fellowship. For love. He doesn't want us to suffer in silence—He wants us to be surrounded by support. You don't have to walk alone. You don't have to cry alone. You don't have to heal alone.

If you're hiding in solitude, let God draw near. He is Emmanuel—God with us. He is the Friend who sticks closer than a brother. He is the Shepherd who leaves the ninety-nine to find the one. You are not forgotten. You are welcome. Let solitude become sanctuary. Let isolation become an invitation. Let your heart be open to love again. You are not alone. You are surrounded. You are welcome.

10. Shattered Dreams

Shattered dreams leave deep wounds. When hopes are crushed, plans fail, or prayers seem unanswered, people lose heart.

SYAVIHA MULENGYA

They stop dreaming. They stop believing. They hide behind the mask of "I'm fine," while grieving silently. They fear disappointment more than anything—so they stop expecting anything.

But God is the restorer of dreams. *"I will restore to you the years the locusts have eaten"* (**Joel 2:25**). He doesn't just heal hearts—He revives hope. He doesn't just mend what's broken—He builds something better. Your dream may be delayed, but it's not denied. People hide behind shattered dreams because they don't want to feel the pain again. They don't want to hope again. They don't want to be let down again. But God invites us to dream again. To believe again. To trust again.

Jesus met people in their disappointment. The woman at the well. The disciples on the road to Emmaus. The man at the pool of Bethesda. He didn't ignore their pain—He transformed it. He turned mourning into dancing, ashes into beauty, and despair into destiny. If you're hiding behind shattered dreams, let God breathe life into your hope. He is the God of resurrection. The God of second chances. The God of new beginnings. You are welcome—not just with your faith, but with your fears

God of Second Chances

Your past may be painful, but it doesn't have to define your future. God is the God of second chances—and third, and fourth, and more. He doesn't give up on you. He doesn't hold your failures against you. He forgives, restores, and renews. *"His mercies are new every morning"* (**Lamentations 3:23**).

Look at Saul. He was a persecutor, feared by many. But when he encountered God, everything changed. He became Paul—a messenger of hope, a builder of churches, a writer of truth. *"If anyone is in Christ, he is a new creation; the old has gone, the new has come"* (**2 Corinthians 5:17**). If God can transform a murderer into a missionary, He can transform you, too.

No mistake is too big for God's mercy. No failure is too final for His forgiveness. He specializes in redemption. He turns broken stories into beautiful testimonies. He turns shame into strength and pain into purpose. *"You turned my mourning into dancing; you removed my sackcloth and clothed me with joy"* (**Psalm 30:11**).

So don't count yourself out. Don't believe the lie that it's too late. With God, it's never too late to start again. He's ready to rewrite your story. And He's waiting for you to say yes. Your past is not your prison—it's the platform for your purpose. Your scars are not signs of defeat—they are symbols of grace.

12

THERE IS HOPE FOR YOU

*****

Mutundi was a man known for his silence. He lived in a small, dusty village where dreams often faded before they began. Life had been hard on him—he had lost his job, his crops had failed, and his family had grown distant. Every morning, he woke up with a heavy heart and questions that had no answers. *"Where is God?"* he wondered. *"If He loves me, why is my life falling apart?"* Doubt became his daily companion, whispering that maybe God had forgotten him.

One day, overwhelmed by frustration, Mutundi sat in his compound staring at the dry, cracked earth. He felt angry—angry at life, at people, and even at God. In a moment of desperation, he grabbed a shovel and began to dig. He didn't know why. Maybe he wanted to bury his pain, or maybe he hoped to find something—anything—that would give him a reason to keep going. He dug for hours, sweat pouring down his face, his hands blistered and sore.

Then, something unexpected happened. His shovel hit something solid. Curious, he cleared the dirt and uncovered a large, old chest. Inside, he found gold—real gold, shining brightly in the sunlight. Mutundi froze. He couldn't believe his eyes. The ground he had walked on for years had hidden treasure beneath it. That moment changed everything. Word spread quickly, and soon the whole village knew: *Mutundi, the quiet man who had struggled for years, had found gold.* He became known as the rich man in town—the man who discovered treasure in the middle of his pain.

But the gold was only part of the story. What truly changed Mutundi was the realization that his doubt had led him to dig, and his digging had led him to discovery. He began to see that sometimes, when life feels dry and hopeless, it's an invitation to search deeper. He found not just wealth, but joy, peace, and restoration. He rebuilt his home, helped others, and found a new purpose. Most of all, he found that God had never left him—He had been waiting for Mutundi to seek.

In the Bible, Thomas doubted that Jesus had risen. He said, *"Unless I see the nail marks in His hands, I will not believe."* But Jesus didn't reject him. He came to Thomas, showed him His hands, and said, *"Stop doubting and believe."* That story reminds us that God is not afraid of our questions. He welcomes them. He meets us in our doubt and gently leads us to faith.

If you are doubting today, remember Mutundi. Remember Thomas. Doubt is not a wall—it can be a doorway. God is not angry with you for asking questions. He invites you to seek Him, and He promises that when you do, you will find Him. Your journey matters. Your questions matter. And most of all, **you are welcome**. "Ask, and it will be given to you; seek, and you will find..." — **Matthew 7:7**

Hope for the Broken

Maha was known in her village for her beauty, kindness, and generosity. She welcomed everyone—rich or poor, stranger or neighbor. Her home was always open, her table always full. She gave without asking, loved without judging, and helped without expecting anything in return. But despite her goodness, rumors began to spread. Some people, jealous of her grace and influence, accused her of being unfaithful. They called her names, whispered behind her back, and labeled her a prostitute. None of it was true. But the lies were loud, and they broke her heart.

The pain of false accusation was deep. Maha stopped attending village gatherings. She avoided the market and walked with her head down. The same people she had fed and comforted now turned away from her. Her name was dragged through the mud, and her soul felt crushed. She cried alone, asking God, *"Why do they hate me? What did I do wrong?"* Her kindness had been misunderstood, and her love had been twisted into shame. Yet, even in her sorrow, she continued to help quietly—feeding hungry children, comforting widows, and praying for those who hurt her.

One day, Maha went to the river, hoping to find peace. She sat by the water, tears falling into the stream. Just then, a young man approached her. He knelt beside her and said, *"Do you remember me?"* Maha looked at him, confused. He smiled and said, *"Years ago, you helped my father and me when we had nothing. You gave us food, shelter, and hope. I never forgot."* That young man had grown into a respected leader in the village. He had heard the lies, but he knew the truth. He stood up for Maha, defended her name, and gave her a second chance. With his help, Maha opened a center for women who had been abused, abandoned, and falsely accused—just like her.

Maha's life was restored. Her name was cleared. Her heart was healed. She became a voice for the voiceless, a shelter for the hurting, and a light for the broken. Her story spread far and wide—

SYAVIHA MULENGYA

not as the woman who was accused, but as the woman who overcame. She taught others that **God receives the accused**, defends the innocent, and turns pain into purpose. Her wounds became her wisdom. Her rejection became her mission. Her work grew, and she helped hundreds of women find healing and hope.

If you feel broken today—falsely accused, abandoned, or ashamed—remember Maha. God sees your heart. He knows the truth. He is near to the brokenhearted and will bind your wounds. Your story is not over. Like Maha, you can rise again. You are welcome. You are loved. You are chosen. "He heals the brokenhearted and binds up their wounds." — **Psalm 147:3**

Healing for the Wounded

All who come are welcome. That includes the wounded— those who are hurting inside, those who carry invisible scars, and those who feel broken by life. Wounds can come from many places: betrayal by someone you trusted, rejection by people you love, failure that crushes your confidence, or loss that leaves you empty. Sometimes, it's not what people did to you, but what they didn't do—like not showing love, not listening, or not standing by you when you needed them most.

God sees all of that. He sees the pain you hide behind your smile. He hears the silent cries you never speak out loud. And He doesn't turn away. He doesn't say, "Come back when you're better." He says, **"Come now, just as you are."** You don't need to be strong to come to God. You don't need to have it all together. In fact, it's your weakness that draws Him closer. He is the Healer of hearts, and He is ready to begin the healing process in you.

Many people believe they must be perfect or "fixed" before they can approach God. But that's not true. God welcomes the wounded first. He is the Great Physician, and He specializes in healing what others cannot see. Whether your wounds are physical, emotional, or spiritual—He understands. He knows your story from beginning to end. He knows what broke you, and He knows how to restore you. His healing is not just about removing pain—it's about giving you peace, strength, and a new beginning.

Healing is not always quick. Sometimes it takes time. But every step you take toward God is a step toward restoration. And as He heals you, something beautiful happens—your story becomes a light for others. Your scars become signs of survival. Your pain becomes a message of hope. God doesn't waste your wounds. He uses them to help others who are hurting. You become a voice of comfort, a source of strength, and a reminder that healing is possible.

So come. Come with your wounds. Come with your tears. Come with your fears and your questions. God is not waiting to judge you—He is waiting to receive you. He is ready to restore what was broken, to renew what was lost, and to rebuild what was torn down. You are not forgotten. You are not too broken. You are welcome. "He heals the brokenhearted and binds up their wounds." — **Psalm 147:3**

Sharing God's Heart for Everyone

God's heart is open to all. He doesn't look at your past, your pain, or your position in life. Whether you've made mistakes, suffered deeply, or feel unworthy, His love remains the same. God welcomes everyone—no matter where they come from or what they've been through. His arms are wide open to the broken, the lost, the confused, and the rejected. He doesn't ask for perfection;

He simply asks you to come. His heart is full of grace, and His desire is to receive you with love and compassion.

Encouraging Boldness to Come to God

Many people hesitate to approach God because they feel ashamed, afraid, or uncertain. But the truth is, God is ready to receive, restore, reveal, and reward those who come to Him. He doesn't push you away—He draws you close. When you come to Him, He begins a beautiful work in your life. He heals your wounds, gives you a new direction, and fills your heart with peace. You don't need to hide or pretend. You can come boldly, knowing that God is faithful and kind. He is waiting to welcome you and walk with you every step of the way.

God is the One who breaks down walls and opens doors. He doesn't wait for you to be perfect before you come to Him. He invites you to come just as you are—with your pain, your questions, your regrets, and your wounds. In His presence, shame is replaced with grace. Fear is replaced with peace. Rejection is replaced with belonging. God's love is not based on your past—it's based on His promise. He sees your heart, and He welcomes you with open arms.

You are not alone. You are not forgotten. You are welcome in God's family. No matter what others have said or how you feel, nothing can separate you from His love. God is ready to restore you, heal you, and give you a new beginning. All who come are welcome—no exceptions. So take that step. Come boldly. Come honestly. Come with hope. God is waiting, and He is ready to receive you.

Love That Welcomes All

God's love is not forced, pressured, or demanding—it is freely given and gently offered. He doesn't push people away because of

SYAVIHA MULENGYA

their past, their pain, or their questions. Instead, He opens His arms wide and says, *"Come."* Whether you are strong or struggling, confident or confused, God's love is for you. He doesn't wait for you to be perfect. He welcomes you as you are. His love is patient, kind, and full of grace. It doesn't judge—it heals. It doesn't shame—it restores. All who come are welcome, and all who come will find love that never fails.

Throughout history and in everyday life, we see stories of transformation—people who were lost and found, broken and healed, rejected and restored. These stories are not just in the Bible; they are happening today. God is still changing lives. He is still lifting people from darkness into light. When you come to Him, He begins a new work in you. He receives you with joy, restores what was broken, reveals your true identity, and rewards your faith. No matter how far you've gone, there is always a way back. And that way is paved with love, mercy, and hope.

This message is not just for believers—it's for seekers, doubters, and those who are curious. You don't need to have all the answers to come to God. You just need to be willing to take a step. Ask questions. Reflect. Explore. God is not afraid of your doubts—He welcomes them. He invites you to discover who He is and how deeply He cares for you. In His presence, you'll find peace, purpose, and a love that transforms. So come. Come with your questions. Come with your pain. Come with your hopes. You are welcome

When You Feel Lost, You Are Still Welcome

Many people feel spiritually discouraged. They carry guilt, shame, and a sense of failure that makes them believe God could never accept them. Maybe you've made choices you regret, drifted away from faith, or feel like you've disappointed God too many times. These feelings whisper, *"You're not good enough,"* or *"God has given up on you."* But those are lies. The truth is, God never stops loving you. His love is not based on your performance—it's based on His promise. He says, *"I have loved you with an everlasting love; I have drawn you with unfailing kindness."* (**Jeremiah 31:3**). If you feel unworthy, know this: **you are still welcome**.

Some people struggle with identity. They don't know who they are or where they belong. The world gives many labels—some painful, some confusing. You may feel lost in your role, your past, or your circumstances. But when you come to God, He gives you a new name: *Loved. Chosen. His.* You are not your mistakes. You are not your pain. You are a child of God, created with purpose and value. The Bible says, *"See what great love the Father has lavished on us, that we should be called children of God! And that is what we are!"* (**1 John 3:1**). In His presence, you don't have to pretend. You can be real, and you can be restored.

Some feel like their situation is beyond hope. They've been through so much that they can't imagine things getting better. The weight of life feels too heavy, and the future seems too dark. But God is the God of new beginnings. He specializes in turning ashes into beauty, sorrow into joy, and brokenness into strength. *"He gives beauty for ashes, the oil of joy for mourning, and a garment of praise for the spirit of heaviness."* (**Isaiah 61:3**). No matter how far you've fallen or how deep the pain, there is always hope in Him. He receives, restores, reveals, and rewards. And He's not just waiting for the strong—He's calling the weary, the wounded, and the wondering.

Sometimes religion or past experiences can make people feel like they don't belong. Maybe you've been judged, hurt, or told you're not good enough. But that's not God's voice. God doesn't shame—He saves. He doesn't reject—He redeems. He doesn't push away—He pulls close. *"Therefore, there is now no condemnation for those who are in Christ Jesus."* (**Romans 8:1**). His heart is open to all who come. He is not looking for perfect people—He is looking for willing hearts. And no matter what others have said, **God says you are welcome**.

Coming to God doesn't mean you have all the answers. It means you're ready to take a step. Ask your questions. Bring your doubts. God is not afraid of your honesty—He welcomes it. He wants a relationship with you, not a performance from you. In His presence, you'll find peace, purpose, and a love that never gives up. *"Draw near to God, and He will draw near to you."* (**James 4:8**). You don't have to fix yourself before you come. Just come.

Hope for Those Struggling in Their Walk with God

There are seasons in life when walking with God feels difficult. You may have started your journey with joy and passion, but now you feel distant, tired, or spiritually dry. Life's pressures, disappointments, and distractions can slowly pull you away from the closeness you once felt. You may even feel guilty for drifting, wondering if God is disappointed in you. But the truth is, **God has not given up on you**. His love is constant, and His grace is greater than your weakness. *"Even if we are faithless, He remains faithful, for He cannot deny Himself."* (**2 Timothy 2:13**).

God understands your struggle. He knows the battles you face, the doubts you carry, and the weariness in your soul. He doesn't condemn you—He invites you back. Just like the father in the story of the prodigal son, God runs toward you with open arms. He longs to restore what was lost and renew what was broken. *"Return to Me, and I will return to you,"* says the Lord in **Malachi 3:7**. His heart

SYAVIHA MULENGYA

is always open to those who come, even if they come limping, broken, or unsure.

Peter's story is a powerful reminder of God's restoring grace. After denying Jesus three times, Peter was filled with shame and sorrow. But Jesus didn't reject him. Instead, He gently restored him and called him to lead. That same grace is available to you. *"The Lord is close to the brokenhearted and saves those who are crushed in spirit."* (**Psalm 34:18**). Your failure is not final. Your weakness is not the end. God sees your heart and your potential, and He is ready to help you rise again.

If you're struggling, take small steps back toward God. You don't need to have everything figured out. Start with a simple prayer. Open your Bible, even if it's just one verse a day. Talk to someone who can encourage you. God is not asking for perfection—He's asking for your heart. *"Draw near to God, and He will draw near to you."* (**James 4:8**). He is patient, kind, and full of mercy. Healing and restoration take time, but every step you take matters.

Shame and guilt often try to keep us away from God. They whisper lies like, *"You're too far gone,"* or *"God won't take you back."* But those lies are not from God. He breaks shame with grace and replaces guilt with forgiveness. *"There is therefore now no condemnation for those who are in Christ Jesus."* (**Romans 8:1**). You are not defined by your past—you are defined by God's love. You are welcome to come back, to be renewed, and to walk again in His light.

So keep walking, even when it's hard. Keep praying, even when words are few. Keep believing, even when your faith feels small.

God is with you. He is for you. And He is ready to restore you. You are not alone. You are not forgotten. You are welcome.

Hope for Those with Strong Faith

If your faith is strong, this book is also for you. Sometimes we think that spiritual maturity means we've arrived. But strong faith is not the end—it's the beginning of deeper growth. God wants to take you further. He wants to reveal more of His heart, His holiness, and His mission for your life. *"Call to Me and I will answer you and tell you great and unsearchable things you do not know."* (**Jeremiah 33:3**). Your strength is a gift, and it's meant to be used—not just for yourself, but for others.

Strong faith brings deeper responsibility. You are called to be a light in dark places, a guide for those who are struggling, and a source of encouragement for the weary. *"Let your light shine before others, that they may see your good deeds and glorify your Father in heaven."* (**Matthew 5:16**). Your walk with God is not just personal—it's purposeful. You are not just called to grow, but to help others grow. Your faith is meant to be shared, lived out, and poured into others.

God rewards those who seek Him with humility and hunger. He reveals His wisdom, His plans, and His power to those who walk closely with Him. But He also calls you to serve with compassion. *"The one who loves God must also love his brother and sister."* (**1 John 4:21**). Your strong faith should lead to strong love—love that lifts, heals, and welcomes. You are called to be a safe place for the hurting and a voice of hope for the doubting.

Let your faith inspire gratitude. Remember where God brought you from. Let it move you to love more deeply, serve more faithfully, and give more generously. Be intentional about mentoring others,

SYAVIHA MULENGYA

praying for the broken, and welcoming those who feel lost. *"Carry each other's burdens, and in this way you will fulfill the law of Christ."* (**Galatians 6:2**). Your strength is not just for you—it's for the body of Christ.

Even with strong faith, there is always more to discover in God. His love is endless, His wisdom is deep, and His presence is life-changing. *"Blessed are those who hunger and thirst for righteousness, for they will be filled."* (**Matthew 5:6**). Keep seeking. Keep growing. Keep welcoming others into the journey. You are not just strong—you are chosen to lead, to love, and to reflect the heart of God.

So whether you are struggling or strong, remember this: **all who come are welcome**. God receives, restores, reveals, and rewards. His love is for everyone—at every stage, in every season. Keep walking. Keep trusting. Keep coming.

13

RUN TO GOD, NOT AWAY FROM HIM

*****

God wants the best for you. He desires to make your life better, beautiful, and blessed. He cares about your happiness, your peace, and your healing. He is not distant or angry—He is near and loving. When you come to Him, you can count on Him. You don't need to hide your pain or pretend to be okay. God sees your tears, understands your struggles, and hears your silent cries. *"Cast all your anxiety on Him because He cares for you."* (**1 Peter 5:7**). He invites you to come as you are, without masks or fear, because He wants to give you what you truly need.

God is your **Savior**—He rescues you from sin, shame, and sorrow. He is your **Supplier**—He provides for your needs, both seen and unseen. He is your **Secret**—He holds the answers to your deepest questions. And He is your **Solution**—He knows how to fix what feels broken. When you run away from Him, you suffer. You struggle with guilt, stress, confusion, and emptiness. You feel stuck, sink deeper into worry, and lose your peace. But when you run to Him, everything begins to change. He doesn't expose you to shame—He covers you with grace. *"The name of the Lord is a strong tower; the righteous run to it and are safe."* (**Proverbs 18:10**).
SYAVIHA MULENGYA

Running to God is not weakness—it's wisdom. He is faithful and trustworthy. He will never reject you or turn you away. He knows your heart and still loves you deeply. When you come to Him, He doesn't remind you of your failures—He reminds you of your future. He lifts you up, strengthens you, and walks with you through every storm. *"Come to Me, all you who are weary and burdened, and I will give you rest."

Why Draw Near to God

1. Savior

God is your Savior. He doesn't wait for you to be perfect—He came to save you while you were still broken. When you run to Him, He doesn't condemn you; He forgives, heals, and restores. Jesus said, *"For the Son of Man came to seek and to save the lost."* (**Luke 19:10**). You don't need to clean yourself up before coming to Him. He saves you just as you are and begins a beautiful transformation from the inside out.

Running away from God leads to guilt, shame, and confusion. But running to Him brings freedom, peace, and joy. He saves you from sin, from fear, and from the lies that try to define you. He gives you a new name, a new heart, and a new beginning. His salvation is not just for eternity—it's for today, for your mind, your emotions, and your relationships.

When you feel lost, don't hide—run to your Savior. He is waiting with open arms. He doesn't expose you to shame; He covers you with grace. He doesn't remind you of your failures; He reminds you of your future. In Him, you are safe, secure, and saved.

2. Supplier

God is your Supplier. Everything you need—peace, strength, wisdom, provision—comes from Him. *"And my God will supply all your needs according to His riches in glory in Christ Jesus."* (**Philippians 4:19**). When you run to Him, you tap into a source that never runs dry. He knows what you need even before you ask, and He delights in providing for His children.

Running away from God leads to emptiness and striving. You try to fill your life with things that don't satisfy. But when you run to Him, He fills your heart, your soul, and your life with abundance. He provides not just material things, but emotional and spiritual nourishment. He gives peace in the storm, joy in sorrow, and hope in uncertainty. God is not limited by your situation. He is generous, faithful, and kind. When you come to Him, you don't have to beg— you simply receive. He is your Provider, your Portion, and your Peace. Run to Him, and you will never be left wanting.

3. Secret

God holds the secrets to your purpose, your healing, and your future. *"The secret of the Lord is with those who fear Him."* (**Psalm 25:14**). When you run to Him, He begins to reveal things that were hidden—truths about who you are, why you were created, and what He has planned for you. He opens your eyes to see beyond your pain and into His promises.

Running away from God keeps you in confusion. You search for answers in people, places, and things, but they never satisfy. When you run to God, He gives you clarity. He speaks to your heart and shows you the way forward. His secrets are not to hide from you— they are treasures waiting to be discovered.

SYAVIHA MULENGYA

God wants to share His heart with you. He wants to reveal His plans, His wisdom, and His love. When you come close, He whispers the truth that sets you free. Don't run from the One who knows everything—run to Him and let Him show you the way.

4. Solution

God is the solution to every problem you face. He is not confused or overwhelmed. He sees the full picture and knows exactly what you need. *"Trust in the Lord with all your heart and lean not on your own understanding."* (**Proverbs 3:5**). When you run to Him, He gives you peace, direction, and answers.

Running away from God leads to stress, struggle, and being stuck. You try to fix things on your own and end up sinking deeper. But when you run to God, He lifts you up. He doesn't just fix your situation—He transforms your heart. He gives wisdom, strength, and grace to walk through every challenge.

God's solution is often Himself. He doesn't just change your circumstances—He changes you. He gives you peace in the waiting, strength in the battle, and joy in the journey. Run to Him, and you'll find the solution you've been searching for.

5. Strengthener

God is your Strengthener. When life feels heavy and you feel weak, He is the one who lifts you up. You don't have to carry everything alone. *"He gives strength to the weary and increases the power of the weak."* (**Isaiah 40:29**). God doesn't just help you survive—He helps you stand, walk, and rise again. His strength is not temporary—it's renewing, restoring, and empowering.

Running away from God when you're tired only makes the burden heavier. But when you run to Him, He gives you rest and refreshes your soul. He strengthens your heart when it's broken, your mind when it's overwhelmed, and your spirit when it's discouraged. *"My flesh and my heart may fail, but God is the strength of my heart and my portion forever."* (**Psalm 73:26**). His strength is perfect in your weakness.

God strengthens you through His Word, His Spirit, and His presence. He gives you the courage to face what you fear and the endurance to keep going. You don't need to be strong to come to Him—you become strong because you came to Him. Run to your Strengthener, and you will find power, peace, and perseverance.

6. Sustainer

God is your Sustainer. He doesn't just start. He holds you together when everything feels like it's falling apart. *"Cast your burden on the Lord, and He will sustain you; He will never let the righteous be shaken."* (**Psalm 55:22**). When you feel like giving up, He gives you grace to keep going.

Running away from God when you're overwhelmed leads to burnout and despair. But running to Him brings renewal. He sustains your faith, your hope, and your joy. He gives you strength for today and hope for tomorrow. He doesn't promise a life without challenges, but He promises to carry you through them. *"Even to your old age and gray hairs I am He, I am He who will sustain you."* (**Isaiah 46:4**).

God sustains you with His presence, His promises, and His peace. He knows what you need and when you need it. He doesn't forget you, and He doesn't fail you. When you feel like you're running away, run to the One who never runs out. He will sustain you with love that never fades.

SYAVIHA MULENGYA

7. Shepherd

God is your Shepherd. He leads you, protects you, and cares for you. *"The Lord is my shepherd; I shall not want."* (**Psalm 23:1**). A shepherd doesn't abandon his sheep—he stays close, watches over them, and guides them to safety. When you run to God, you run to someone who knows the way and walks with you.

Running away from God leads to confusion and danger. Like sheep without a shepherd, we wander and get lost. But when you run to Him, He brings you back to the right path. He doesn't scold you—He gently restores you. *"He tends His flock like a shepherd: He gathers the lambs in His arms and carries them close to His heart."* (**Isaiah 40:11**). You are never too far for Him to find you.

God's guidance is gentle and wise. He leads you beside still waters and restores your soul. He walks with you through valleys and celebrates with you on mountaintops. Run to your Shepherd, and you will never walk alone.

8. Shield

God is your Shield. He protects you from harm, defends you from attacks, and covers you with His presence. *"But You, Lord, are a shield around me, my glory, the One who lifts my head high."* (**Psalm 3:3**). When you run to Him, you run into safety. He surrounds you with peace and guards your heart.

Running away from God leaves you exposed to fear, anxiety, and spiritual attacks. But when you run to Him, you are covered. His Word becomes your armor, and His Spirit becomes your defender. *"Every word of God is flawless; He is a shield to those who take refuge in Him."* (**Proverbs 30:5**). You don't have to fight alone—He fights for you.

God's protection is powerful and personal. He doesn't just shield you from danger—He shields you from despair. He lifts your head when you're discouraged and gives you confidence when you feel afraid. Run to your Shield, and you will find peace, protection, and strength.

SYAVIHA MULENGYA

14

YOU ARE A WINNER DESPITE YOUR WEAKNESS AND WORRY

*****

1. David – The Fallen but Favored

The Fallen but Favored

Failure: David was chosen by God and anointed as king, yet he made a terrible mistake. He committed adultery with Bathsheba and arranged the death of her husband, Uriah (**2 Samuel 11**). His actions brought sorrow, shame, and consequences to his family and kingdom. But David didn't hide or justify his sin—he confessed it with a broken heart. He said, "Against You, You only, have I sinned" (**Psalm 51:4**). His failure was serious, but it was not the end of his story.

Forgiveness and Faith: When David repented, he didn't just say sorry—he pleaded for a clean heart and a renewed spirit (**Psalm 51:10**). God heard his cry and forgave him, showing that mercy is greater than mistakes. David's faith remained strong even after his fall. He continued to trust in God's goodness and grace. His psalms became songs of healing for generations. David teaches us that forgiveness is available to those who come with humility.

Fervor and Favor: David's love for God was deep and passionate. He danced before the Lord with joy, unashamed of his worship (**2 Samuel 6:14**). His fervor for God's presence never faded, even in hard times. Because of his heart, God gave him favor and promised that his throne would last forever (2 Samuel 7:16). David's story reminds us that God welcomes the broken and uses them for great things. Even the fallen can be favored when they return to God with faith and fervor,

2. Peter – The Denier but Delivered

Doubt: Peter was bold, yet often uncertain. He walked on water but began to sink when he doubted (**Matthew 14:30**). His heart was sincere, but fear made him stumble. He promised to stand with Jesus, yet denied Him three times (**Luke 22:61**). That moment broke him, and he wept bitterly. Doubt had shaken his confidence, but not his calling.

Denial and Despair: Peter's denial was public and painful. He had failed the One he loved most. But Jesus didn't reject him— instead, He restored him gently (**John 21:15-17**). Jesus asked, "Do you love Me?" three times, healing Peter's shame. That conversation turned despair into devotion. Peter was not disqualified; he was re-commissioned.

Devotion and Destiny: Peter became a powerful preacher, leading thousands to Christ (**Acts 2:41**). His devotion grew stronger through grace. He wrote letters that still encourage believers today (**1 Peter, 2 Peter**). His destiny was not destroyed by denial. God used him to build the church. Peter's life proves that grace rewrites failure into faithfulness.

SYAVIHA MULENGYA

3. Rahab – The Prostitute but Protected

Past: Rahab lived in Jericho and worked as a prostitute (**Joshua 2:1**). Her lifestyle was sinful, and her reputation was shameful. But when she heard about the God of Israel, she believed. She welcomed the spies and hid them, putting her life at risk. Her faith was stronger than her past. She said, "The Lord your God is God in heaven" (**Joshua 2:11**).

Protection and Promise: Because of her courage, Rahab and her family were spared when Jericho fell (**Joshua 6:25**). She hung a scarlet cord in her window—a symbol of salvation. God honored her faith and protected her from destruction. She didn't just survive—she was welcomed into God's people. Her story became part of His promise.

Purpose and Praise: Rahab married into Israel and became an ancestor of Jesus (**Matthew 1:5**). Her life was transformed from shame to significance. She is praised in **Hebrews 11** as a woman of faith (**Hebrews 11:31**). God gave her a new purpose and a lasting legacy. Rahab shows us that no one is too far gone for God's grace.

4. Ruth – The Rejected but Redeemed

Refugee: Ruth was a widow from Moab, a land often looked down upon by Israel (**Ruth 1:4**). She had lost her husband, her home, and her security. Yet she chose to follow Naomi and embrace the God of Israel. Her decision was bold and full of faith. She said, "Your God will be my God" (**Ruth 1:16**). Though she was a refugee, she was not forgotten by God.

Resilience and Risk: Ruth worked hard in the fields, gathering leftover grain to survive (**Ruth 2:2**). She didn't complain—she kept going with quiet strength. Her resilience opened doors to favor with Boaz, a kind and godly man. Ruth also took a risk by approaching

Boaz at night, asking him to redeem her (**Ruth 3:9).** Her courage was rewarded with love, protection, and a new beginning.

Redemption and Royalty: Boaz married Ruth and redeemed her story (**Ruth 4:13**). She became the great-grandmother of King David and part of Jesus' family line (**Matthew 1:5**). Ruth's journey from rejection to royalty shows God's power to restore. He welcomes those who feel like outsiders. Her life teaches us that faith and loyalty can lead to redemption and honor.

5. Moses – The Fugitive but Faithful

Moses began his life in Pharaoh's palace, raised with privilege and power. But after killing an Egyptian in anger (**Exodus 2:12**), he fled into the wilderness, living in fear and isolation for forty years. He felt unworthy, unsure, and forgotten. When God called him from the burning bush, Moses asked, "Who am I that I should go?" (**Exodus 3:11**). His fear made him question his identity and ability. Yet God saw beyond his weakness and spoke with purpose, reminding him, "I will be with you" (**Exodus 3:12**).

Though Moses gave excuses—"I am not eloquent" (**Exodus 4:10**)—God didn't give up on him. Instead, He revealed His power through fire and His presence through promise. That encounter marked a turning point. Moses moved from failure to faith, from hiding to leading. He obeyed, faced Pharaoh, and became a vessel of miracles. God used him to part the Red Sea (**Exodus 14:21**), bring water from a rock (**Exodus 17:6**), and deliver the Ten Commandments (**Exodus 20:1–17**). His obedience unlocked freedom for a nation.

Moses' story reminds us that God calls the unlikely to do the impossible. You may feel unqualified, but God equips those He calls. He doesn't ask for perfection—He asks for surrender. If you've been hiding in fear, it's time to step forward in faith. **Reflection Questions**: What excuses have you been giving God? Where do you need to trust His presence more than your ability? Are you willing to say yes, even if you feel afraid?

6. Jacob – The Deceiver but Delivered

Jacob's name meant "supplanter," and he lived up to it. He tricked his father and stole his brother's blessing (**Genesis 27:35**), then ran away in fear. His life was marked by manipulation, guilt, and shame. Yet God didn't abandon him. In a dream, Jacob saw a ladder reaching to heaven (**Genesis 28:12**), and God said, "I am with you and will watch over you" (**Genesis 28:15**). Even in deceit, God extended grace.

Years later, Jacob wrestled with God all night (**Genesis 32:24**). He refused to let go until he was blessed. That struggle was not just physical—it was spiritual. God changed his name to Israel, saying, "You have struggled with God and with humans and have overcome" (**Genesis 32:28**). Jacob moved from deceit to dependence, from fear to faith. His destiny was shaped through discipline and surrender.

Jacob became the father of twelve tribes—the foundation of Israel. His life was transformed by God's mercy. He learned that true strength comes from clinging to God, not controlling others. If you've lived with regret or manipulation, God can still deliver you. **Reflection Questions**: What are you wrestling with today? Are you willing to let go of control and hold on to God? How has God used your struggles to shape your story?

7. Paul – The Persecutor but Preacher

Paul, once called Saul, was proud and powerful. He persecuted Christians and approved their deaths (**Acts 8:3**), thinking he was
SYAVIHA MULENGYA

serving God. His pride blinded him to the truth. But on the road to Damascus, Jesus stopped him with a blinding light and said, "Saul, Saul, why do you persecute Me?" (**Acts 9:4**). That moment shattered his pride and opened his eyes to grace.

Paul was struck blind and spent three days in prayer and fasting (**Acts 9:9**). God sent Ananias to heal him and baptize him. Saul became Paul—a new man with a new mission. He was pursued by grace, not punishment. He preached boldly, planted churches, and wrote letters that continue to shape the Christian faith today. He declared, "*I am not ashamed of the gospel*" (**Romans 1:16**). His pain became the path to purpose.

Paul's life proves that no one is too far gone for God. Grace transforms even the hardest heart. If you've hurt others or lived in pride, God can still use you. He doesn't waste your past—He redeems it. **Reflection Questions**: What part of your past do you think disqualifies you? How has God pursued you with grace? Are you ready to turn your pain into purpose?

8. Esther – The Orphan but Ordained

Esther lost her parents and was raised by her cousin Mordecai (**Esther 2:7**). She grew up quietly, without status or power. Yet God had a plan for her life. Though she was an orphan, she was not overlooked. God placed her in the palace for a purpose. Her story began in silence but ended in strength. She was chosen "for such a time as this" (**Esther 4:14**).

Esther obeyed Mordecai's advice and kept her identity hidden (**Esther 2:10**). When danger came, she didn't run—she rose. She said, "If I perish, I perish" (**Esther 4:16**), showing courage and faith. Her obedience opened the door to opportunity. God used her to save the Jewish people. Her boldness changed history and protected generations.

Esther's life teaches us that God positions us for purpose. You may feel unseen or unqualified, but God sees you and has placed you exactly where you need to be. Your voice matters. Your courage counts. **Reflection Questions**: What fear is holding you back from speaking up? Where has God placed you "for such a time as this?" Are you willing to rise and risk for the sake of others?

Overcoming and Offering: Esther overcame fear and used her position to protect others. She didn't seek glory—she offered her life for her people. Her story reminds us that God uses the humble and hidden. He ordains those who feel forgotten. Esther's life teaches us that obedience leads to impact. Even orphans can become queens in God's plan.

9. The Samaritan Woman – The Shamed but Saved

Shame: She came to the well at noon, avoiding others (**John 4:6**). Her past was painful—five husbands and a broken reputation. She felt unworthy and unwanted. But Jesus met her there, not with judgment, but with love. He spoke to her gently and truthfully. Her shame didn't stop Him from offering salvation.

Search and Savior: She was searching for water, but Jesus offered her living water (**John 4:10**). He revealed her story and still welcomed her. She said, "Come see a man who told me everything I ever did" (**John 4:29**). Her encounter with Jesus changed her life. She found the Savior she didn't know she needed. Her thirst was finally satisfied.

Spirit and Story: Jesus filled her with truth and Spirit. She became the first evangelist in her town. Her story, once filled with shame, became a testimony of grace. She didn't hide anymore—
SYAVIHA MULENGYA

she shared boldly. God used her brokenness to bring healing to others. Her life shows that Jesus meets us in our mess and gives us a message.

10. Hannah – The Barren but Blessed

Brokenness: Hannah was deeply hurt because she couldn't have children (**1 Samuel 1:6**). She was mocked and misunderstood. Her heart was heavy with sorrow. Yet she didn't give up—she went to God in prayer. She poured out her soul with tears and honesty (**1 Samuel 1:10**). Her brokenness became her offering.

Boldness and Belief Hannah prayed with boldness and made a vow to God (**1 Samuel 1:11**). She believed that God could change her situation. Eli, the priest, thought she was drunk, but she was praying with passion. God heard her cry and answered her request. She gave birth to Samuel, a prophet and leader. Her belief brought a breakthrough.

Birth and Blessing Hannah kept her promise and gave Samuel to serve God (**1 Samuel 1:28**). She didn't hold back—she gave her best. God blessed her with more children later (**1 Samuel 2:21**). Her story is one of faith, sacrifice, and joy. Hannah teaches us that prayer works and promises matter. From barrenness came blessing and legacy.

11. The Woman in Adultery – The Accused but Accepted

Accusation: The woman was caught in the act of adultery and dragged before Jesus by religious leaders (**John 8:3**). She was exposed publicly, humiliated, and used as a trap to test Jesus. The law said she should be stoned, but her accusers were not seeking justice—they were seeking to condemn. She stood alone, ashamed and afraid, surrounded by judgment. Her sin was real, but so was the cruelty of those who condemned her. She was accused, but Jesus saw more than her mistake.

Acceptance and Advocacy: Jesus didn't respond with harshness—He responded with wisdom and compassion. He bent down and wrote in the dust, then said, "Let the one who has never sinned throw the first stone" (**John 8:7**). One by one, her accusers walked away, convicted by their own conscience. Jesus stood up and asked, "Where are your accusers?" She replied, "No one, Lord." Then He said, "Neither do I condemn you. Go and sin no more" (**John 8:11**). Jesus didn't excuse her sin—He offered her a new beginning.

Awakening and Assignment: This woman came to Jesus in shame but left in freedom. She was not defined by her past—she was invited into a future. Jesus awakened her to grace, truth, and transformation. He didn't just protect her—He empowered her to change. Her story reminds us that mercy triumphs over judgment. When we come to Jesus, we are not cast out—we are called up. Even the accused can be accepted when they meet the Advocate.

God's Word is full of stories that remind us: no one is too far gone for grace. David failed through sin, yet found forgiveness and favor because he repented with a sincere heart (**Psalm 51**). Ruth was a rejected foreigner, but her loyalty and faith led her into redemption and royalty (**Ruth 4:13; Matthew 1:5**). Peter denied Jesus in fear, but was restored and became a bold preacher (**John 21:15–17; Acts 2:41**). Rahab lived in sin, yet her faith saved her family and placed her in the lineage of Christ (**Joshua 6:25; Matthew 1:5**). These lives show that God does not look for perfection—He looks for honesty, humility, and a heart that turns toward Him.

SYAVIHA MULENGYA

Moses ran from his past, but God called him through fire and used him to lead a nation to freedom (**Exodus 3:2; 14:21**). Jacob deceived his family, yet God gave him a new name and destiny after a night of wrestling (**Genesis 32:28**). Paul persecuted believers, but Jesus met him on the road and turned him into a powerful preacher (**Acts 9:4; Romans 1:16**). Esther was an orphan, but God placed her in the palace to protect His people (**Esther 4:14**). These stories remind us that God sees beyond our weakness and welcomes us into His work. He transforms fugitives into leaders, deceivers into fathers of nations, and persecutors into proclaimers of truth.

The Samaritan woman came to the well in shame, but Jesus offered her living water and turned her into a witness (**John 4:10, 29**). Hannah was barren and broken, but her bold prayers brought birth and blessing (**1 Samuel 1:10, 20**). The woman caught in adultery was publicly accused, yet Jesus defended her and gave her a new beginning (**John 8:11**). These women were not rejected— they were restored. Jesus did not condemn them; He called them to rise. Their stories show that God meets us in our mess, speaks truth with love, and sends us out with purpose.

The message is clear: all who come are welcome. Whether you are broken like David, bold like Ruth, burdened like Hannah, or bruised like the woman in adultery—God says, "Come." Jesus declared, "Whoever comes to Me I will never cast out" (**John 6:37**). He is the Savior who forgives, the Shepherd who guides, and the Shield who protects. Your past does not disqualify you—your willingness to come opens the door to healing, hope, and a new beginning. So come with your pain, your questions, your failures, and your faith. God is waiting—not to punish you, but to welcome you home.

SYAVIHA MULENGYA

15

BE A FRIEND OF GOD, DO NOT BE AFRAID OF HIM

*****

Mupesa's Invitation — From Fear to Friendship with God

Mupesa was a woman known for her quiet strength and independence. She lived a life that many judged from the outside—colorful, complicated, and far from what people considered "holy." One day, she received an invitation to a fundraising event. She accepted without hesitation, wanting to support the cause. On the day of the event, she dressed modestly, entered the address into her GPS, and followed the directions. But as she arrived, her heart sank—the GPS had led her to a church.

She froze. Her hands trembled as she reached for her phone and called the organizer. "I'm sorry," she said, "I didn't know this was happening in a church. I can't come in. I know who I am. I know the life I've lived. I'm afraid of God. If I enter that place, He might punish me." Her voice cracked. "If I go in, I'll have to ask for forgiveness—but I don't even know if He'll accept it." Her words were heavy with shame, fear, and deep pain.

SYAVIHA MULENGYA

The organizer handed the phone to the pastor, who happened to be nearby. His voice was calm and kind. "Mupesa," he said, "don't be afraid of God. Be a friend of God." She was stunned. "A friend?" she asked. "How can a sinner like me be a friend of a holy God?" The pastor replied gently, "God is looking for sinners. Not perfect people. Not the righteous. He came for people like you and me." She hesitated. "Not like me," she whispered. "I'm the worst of them all." But the pastor didn't give up. He spoke with compassion, reminding her of the story of the prodigal son, the woman caught in adultery, and Peter, who denied Jesus, and how each one was received with love, not rejection.

Moved by his words, Mupesa agreed to enter the church compound—but she asked to stay outside the sanctuary. She sat quietly on a bench near the entrance, watching others go in. Her heart was pounding, but something inside her began to soften. She listened to the music, the prayers, and the message. Tears rolled down her cheeks. She didn't feel judged. She felt seen. She didn't feel condemned. She felt invited. That day, she didn't walk into the church building—but she walked into the beginning of healing.

Why We Should Not Be Afraid of God

Mupesa's story is a beautiful reminder that God is not standing at the gates of heaven with a list of our failures, waiting to punish us. Instead, He is standing with open arms, longing to welcome us home. Too many people walk through life burdened by fear, guilt, and shame, convinced they've strayed too far or fallen too hard to be embraced by divine love. But that's a lie that keeps hearts locked in isolation. The truth is, God's heart beats passionately for the broken, the lost, and the hurting. He is not searching for flawless perfection—He is seeking honest hearts that are willing to come as

SYAVIHA MULENGYA

they are. Mupesa's journey shows us that no matter how far we've wandered, we are never beyond the reach of grace.

God is not your harsh judge, waiting to condemn you. He is your Savior, your Rescuer, your Redeemer. He doesn't point fingers—He extends hands. He is your Supplier, the One who provides peace in chaos, hope in despair, and strength in weakness. He holds the secrets to your healing, the solutions to your struggles, and the strategies for your restoration. When you feel weak, He becomes your Strengthener. When you're weary, He becomes your Sustainer. When you're lost, He becomes your Shepherd. And when fear surrounds you, He becomes your Shield. Every name He bears reflects a need He meets.

So don't run away from God—run to Him. Don't hide your wounds—hand them over. He will not expose you to shame; He will envelop you in grace. He will not reject you for your past; He will redeem you for your future. Like Mupesa, you may feel unworthy, broken, or burdened, but God's invitation is simple and profound: "Come as you are." There is no prerequisite for perfection, no requirement for righteousness—just a willingness to be real. And when you come, you'll discover that the love you feared was out of reach has been chasing you all along.

God's love is not earned—it's extended. It's not reserved for the righteous—it's poured out for the repentant. His grace is not a reward for good behavior; it's a rescue for those drowning in despair. Mupesa's story is not just a testimony—it's a mirror. It reflects the truth that every soul, no matter how stained or scarred, is precious to God. He doesn't discard the damaged; He delights in restoring them. He doesn't shame the sinner; He showers them with mercy. And He doesn't wait for us to be ready—He simply waits for us to respond.

SYAVIHA MULENGYA

When you come to God, you don't just find forgiveness—you find family. You don't just receive mercy—you receive meaning. You don't just escape judgment—you enter joy. Mupesa's transformation is proof that God specializes in turning messes into messages, trials into testimonies, and pain into purpose. The same God who welcomed Mupesa is waiting to welcome you. Not with a lecture, but with love. Not with condemnation, but with compassion. Not with rejection, but with restoration.

So today, let Mupesa's story stir something in your soul. Let it remind you that you are not too far gone, not too broken, not too late. God's arms are open, His heart is full, and His voice is calling. "Come as you are." And when you do, you'll realize that the journey back to God is not a path of punishment—it's a pathway to peace, healing, and hope

1. Call on God

Calling on God is the first step in building a relationship with Him. He is not a distant figure waiting to judge you—He is a loving Father who wants to hear your voice. The Bible says, *"Call to me and I will answer you and tell you great and unsearchable things you do not know"* (**Jeremiah 33:3**). This is a promise, not a possibility. God is always available.

You don't need to be perfect to call on God. You don't need fancy words or a special place. Just speak from your heart. Whether you whisper, shout, or cry, God hears you. **Psalm 145:18** says, *"The Lord is near to all who call on him, to all who call on him in truth."* He listens with love and responds with wisdom.

Calling on God is an act of faith. It shows that you believe He is real, powerful, and caring. **Romans 10:13** says, *"Everyone who calls on the name of the Lord will be saved."* That means you are never too far gone, never too broken, and never too late to reach out to Him.

When you call on God, you invite Him into your situation. You allow Him to work in your life. He may not always answer the way you expect, but He always answers in the best way. His timing is perfect, and His plans are good.

Make calling on God a daily habit. Talk to Him in the morning, during your work, and before you sleep. Let Him be your first call, not your last resort. He wants to walk with you through every moment of your life. So don't be afraid—call on God. He's waiting to hear from you. He loves you more than you can imagine, and He's ready to respond with grace, peace, and power.

2. Cast Your Worry to Him

Worry is a heavy burden, but God never meant for you to carry it alone. He invites you to give Him your fears, doubts, and stress. *"Cast all your anxiety on him because he cares for you"* (**1 Peter 5:7**). This is not just comforting—it's life-changing.

When you cast your worries on God, you're choosing trust over fear. You're saying, "God, I believe You can handle this better than I can." That's a powerful declaration of faith. **Philippians 4:6-7** says, *"Do not be anxious about anything...present your requests to God. And the peace of God...will guard your hearts."*

God's shoulders are strong enough to carry your heaviest burdens. He doesn't get tired, overwhelmed, or frustrated. He is your refuge and strength, an ever-present help in trouble (**Psalm 46:1**). You can rest in His care.

Casting your worries doesn't mean ignoring your problems. It means facing them with God by your side. It means praying, trusting, and letting go of control. Jesus said, *"Come to me, all you who are weary and burdened, and I will give you rest"* (**Matthew 11:28**).

You may need to cast your worries again and again. That's okay. God never gets tired of hearing from you. He never says, "You've come too many times." His love is endless, and His patience is perfect.

So take a deep breath. Whatever is troubling you—give it to God. He's not just able to help; He's eager to help. Let Him carry your load and fill your heart with peace.

3. Count on Him

God is trustworthy. You can count on Him when everything else fails. People may disappoint you, plans may fall apart, but God remains faithful. *"Trust in the Lord with all your heart and lean not on your own understanding"* (**Proverbs 3:5**). His wisdom is greater than ours.

Counting on God means relying on His promises. He has never broken a promise and never will. **Lamentations 3:22-23** says, *"Because of the Lord's great love we are not consumed...great is your faithfulness."* His love is constant, and His mercy is new every morning.

Even when life is confusing, God is working behind the scenes. **Romans 8:28** reminds us, *"In all things God works for the good of those who love him."* You may not see the full picture, but God does. He's weaving your story with purpose.

To count on God is to rest in His character. He is good, kind, just, and loving. He doesn't change with circumstances. **Hebrews 13:8** says, *"Jesus Christ is the same yesterday and today and* *forever."* That means you can trust Him today, tomorrow, and always.

Sometimes counting on God means waiting. It means believing even when the answer hasn't come. **Isaiah 40:31** says, *"But those who hope in the Lord will renew their strength."* Waiting with faith brings strength, not weakness.

So lean on Him. Count on His love, His power, and His timing. He will never let you down. He is your anchor in the storm and your light in the darkness.

4. Confess to Him

Confession is not about guilt—it's about grace. God already knows your mistakes, but He wants you to bring them to Him. *"If we confess our sins, he is faithful and just and will forgive us...and purify us"* (**1 John 1:9**). That's the beauty of forgiveness. When you confess, you're not condemned—you're cleansed. You're saying, "God, I need Your mercy." **Psalm 32:5** says, *"I acknowledged my sin to you...and you forgave the guilt of my sin."* Confession opens the door to healing and restoration.

God doesn't reject you when you're honest. He embraces you. Like the father in the story of the prodigal son (**Luke 15**), He runs to you with open arms. He rejoices when you return to Him. His love is greater than your failures.

Confession brings freedom. It removes the weight of shame and replaces it with peace. David said in **Psalm 51:10**, *"Create in me a pure heart, O God, and renew a steadfast spirit within me."* God doesn't just forgive—He transforms.

You don't need to hide from God. He sees everything and still loves you. **Hebrews 4:13** says, *"Nothing in all creation is hidden* *from God's sight."* So come boldly, not fearfully. He is ready to forgive and restore. Make confession a regular part of your walk with God. It keeps your heart clean and your relationship strong. God is not angry—He is loving. He wants to heal your wounds and walk with you in grace.

5. Consult Him

God is the best advisor you'll ever have. He knows your future, understands your past, and sees your heart. *"If any of you lacks wisdom, you should ask God...who gives generously"* (**James 1:5**). He's ready to guide you. Consulting God means seeking His opinion before making decisions. It's saying, "Lord, what do You think?" **Proverbs 16:3** says, *"Commit to the Lord whatever you do, and he will establish your plans."* His wisdom is perfect, and His guidance is sure.

God speaks through His Word, His Spirit, and godly counsel. He doesn't leave you guessing. **Psalm 32:8** promises, *"I will instruct you and teach you in the way you should go."* He is your personal guide, always available.

When you consult God, you avoid many mistakes. You gain clarity, peace, and direction. **Isaiah 30:21** says, *"Whether you turn to the right or to the left, your ears will hear a voice...saying, 'This is the way; walk in it.'"* God's voice leads you to life.

Don't wait until things go wrong to seek God's advice. Ask Him first. Involve Him in your plans, dreams, and decisions. He cares about every detail of your life.

So before you move, pray. Before you choose, ask. God's advice is always right—and always available. He wants to walk with you and lead you into His perfect will.

SYAVIHA MULENGYA

6. Come to Him Anytime, Anywhere

God is not limited by time, place, or circumstance. You can come to Him in the morning, at night, in joy, in sorrow, in silence, or in song. **Hebrews 4:16** encourages us, *"Let us then approach God's throne of grace with confidence, so that we may receive mercy and find grace to help us in our time of need."* This means you are always welcome in His presence.

You don't need a church building or a special ritual to meet with God. He is everywhere. **Psalm 139:7-10** says, *"Where can I go from your Spirit? Where can I flee from your presence?"* Whether you're in a crowded place or alone in your room, God is near. He is not far from anyone who seeks Him.

Coming to God anytime means living in constant communion with Him. It's not just about scheduled prayers—it's about a lifestyle of connection.

You can talk to Him while walking, working, cooking, or resting. He listens to every word, every sigh, and every thought. God doesn't require perfection to approach Him. He invites you as you are. Jesus said, *"Come to me, all you who are weary and burdened, and I will give you rest"* (When you come to God, you receive strength, peace, and direction. You are reminded that you are not alone. **Isaiah 41:10** says, *"Do not fear, for I am with you… I will strengthen you and help you."* His presence brings comfort and courage. So come to Him, anytime, anywhere. In joy or pain, in clarity or confusion, He is ready to receive you. He is your safe place, your constant companion, and your faithful friend.

7. Cry to Him

Crying to God is not a weakness—it's a powerful expression of trust. When you cry to God, you're not just releasing emotion;

SYAVIHA MULENGYA

you're reaching out to the One who understands you completely. **Psalm 34:17-18** says, *"The righteous cry out, and the Lord hears them; he delivers them from all their troubles. The Lord is close to the brokenhearted and saves those who are crushed in spirit."* God is not distant from your pain—He is present in it.

Tears are a language God understands. Even when you can't find the words, your tears speak volumes. **Psalm 56:8** says, *"You keep track of all my sorrows. You have collected all my tears in your bottle. You have recorded each one in your book."* This shows how deeply God cares. He doesn't ignore your pain—He treasures your tears.

Crying to God is an act of surrender. It's saying, "God, I can't do this on my own." And that's exactly where His strength begins. **2 Corinthians 12:9** reminds us, *"My grace is sufficient for you, for my power is made perfect in weakness."* When you cry out, you invite God's power into your situation.

Many great men and women in the Bible cried to God. David cried in the wilderness. Hannah wept in the temple. Jesus Himself wept at the tomb of Lazarus. Crying is not a sign of failure—it's a sign of faith. It shows that you believe God is listening and that He cares enough to respond.

Sometimes, your cry may be silent. Other times, it may be loud and desperate. Either way, God hears. He doesn't need you to be strong—He just needs you to be honest. **Psalm 18:6** says, _"In my distress I called to the Lord.

Confession and Surrender

Heavenly Father, I come before You with a heart that's heavy and honest. I confess my sins—my pride, my fear, my failures. I've tried to do life my way, and I've stumbled. Forgive me, Lord, for the

SYAVIHA MULENGYA

times I ignored Your voice, for the moments I chose comfort over calling, and for the wounds I caused by words or silence.

Wash me clean. Renew my mind. Restore my joy.

I surrender all—my plans, my pain, my past. Let Your grace rewrite my story. Let Your mercy mend what's broken. Let Your Spirit lead me from this day forward. In Jesus' name, **Amen.**

Prayer 2: Invitation to Jesus

Lord Jesus, I open the door of my heart to You. Come in—not just as a guest, but as King. I believe You died for me, rose for me, and live to love me. I receive Your gift of salvation, Your promise of peace, and Your power to transform.

Make me new. Make me bold. Make me Yours.

Fill me with Your Spirit. Teach me to walk in Your ways. Use me to bring hope to others. From this moment on, I belong to You. In Your holy name, **Amen.**

BY SYAVIHA MULENGYA

www.ingramcontent.com/pod-product-compliance
Lightning Source LLC
Chambersburg PA
CBHW071515120626
46550CB00006B/2228